Current
CONTROVERSIES

Patriotism

Other Books in the Current Controversies Series

Patriotism

Sylvia Engdahl, Book Editor

GREENHAVEN PRESS
A part of Gale, Cengage Learning

Detroit • New York • San Francisco • New Haven, Conn • Waterville, Maine • London

Christine Nasso, *Publisher*
Elizabeth Des Chenes, *Managing Editor*

© 2011 Greenhaven Press, a part of Gale, Cengage Learning

Articles in Greenhaven Press anthologies are often edited for length to meet page requirements. In addition, original titles of these works are changed to clearly present the main thesis and to explicitly indicate the author's opinion. Every effort is made to ensure that Greenhaven Press accurately reflects the original intent of the authors. Every effort has been made to trace the owners of copyrighted material.

Cover image copyright © Encore/Alamy.

LIBRARY OF CONGRESS CATALOGING-IN-PUBLICATION DATA

Patriotism / Sylvia Engdahl, book editor.
 p. cm. -- (Current controversies)
 Includes bibliographical references and index.
 ISBN 978-0-7377-4921-2 (hbk.) -- ISBN 978-0-7377-4922-9 (pbk.)
 1. Patriotism--United States. I. Engdahl, Sylvia.
 JK1759.P355 2011
 323.6'50973--dc22
                                                    2010050556

Printed in the United States of America
1 2 3 4 5 6 7 15 14 13 12 11

Contents

In a speech before the House of Representatives, Congressman Ron Paul argues that patriotism also includes the effort to resist government oppression. Opponents of government policies are often called unpatriotic; however, it is frequently the actions of those dissenters that preserve our personal liberties.

The ideals upon which America was founded have disappeared in today's more cynical generation. The concept of patriotism has been cheapened and used in destructive ways. It is time to return to the principles of service to the country and concern about the future that made America great in the past.

Chapter 2: Is Patriotism on the Decline?

Chapter 4: Should Flag Burning Be Banned by Law?

No: The Flag Symbolizes Americans' Right to Freedom of Expression

Foreword

By definition, controversies are "discussions of questions in which opposing opinions clash" (Webster's Twentieth Century Dictionary Unabridged). Few would deny that controversies are a pervasive part of the human condition and exist on virtually every level of human enterprise. Controversies transpire between individuals and among groups, within nations and between nations. Controversies supply the grist necessary for progress by providing challenges and challengers to the status quo. They also create atmospheres where strife and warfare can flourish. A world without controversies would be a peaceful world; but it also would be, by and large, static and prosaic.

The Series' Purpose

The purpose of the Current Controversies series is to explore many of the social, political, and economic controversies dominating the national and international scenes today. Titles selected for inclusion in the series are highly focused and specific. For example, from the larger category of criminal justice, Current Controversies deals with specific topics such as police brutality, gun control, white collar crime, and others. The debates in Current Controversies also are presented in a useful, timeless fashion. Articles and book excerpts included in each title are selected if they contribute valuable, long-range ideas to the overall debate. And wherever possible, current information is enhanced with historical documents and other relevant materials. Thus, while individual titles are current in focus, every effort is made to ensure that they will not become quickly outdated. Books in the Current Controversies series will remain important resources for librarians, teachers, and students for many years.

In addition to keeping the titles focused and specific, great care is taken in the editorial format of each book in the series. Book introductions and chapter prefaces are offered to provide background material for readers. Chapters are organized around several key questions that are answered with diverse opinions representing all points on the political spectrum. Materials in each chapter include opinions in which authors clearly disagree as well as alternative opinions in which authors may agree on a broader issue but disagree on the possible solutions. In this way, the content of each volume in Current Controversies mirrors the mosaic of opinions encountered in society. Readers will quickly realize that there are many viable answers to these complex issues. By questioning each author's conclusions, students and casual readers can begin to develop the critical thinking skills so important to evaluating opinionated material.

Current Controversies is also ideal for controlled research. Each anthology in the series is composed of primary sources taken from a wide gamut of informational categories including periodicals, newspapers, books, US and foreign government documents, and the publications of private and public organizations. Readers will find factual support for reports, debates, and research papers covering all areas of important issues. In addition, an annotated table of contents, an index, a book and periodical bibliography, and a list of organizations to contact are included in each book to expedite further research.

Perhaps more than ever before in history, people are confronted with diverse and contradictory information. During the Persian Gulf War, for example, the public was not only treated to minute-to-minute coverage of the war, it was also inundated with critiques of the coverage and countless analyses of the factors motivating US involvement. Being able to sort through the plethora of opinions accompanying today's major issues, and to draw one's own conclusions, can be a complicated and frustrating struggle. It is the editors' hope that Current Controversies will help readers with this struggle.

Introduction

> *"Among the chief values of patriotism is that in times of trouble it can unite people and give them a sense of belonging to something larger than themselves . . . "*

Most people have a firm picture in their minds of what patriotism is, and on the basis of this picture, they are quick to judge whether other people are less patriotic than they are. Many would be surprised to hear that various forms of patriotism exist and that not everyone agrees about what it means to be patriotic. As Mark Twain wrote, "Each must for himself alone decide what is right and what is wrong, and which course is patriotic and which isn't."[1]

Until fairly recently, patriotism was a subject involving strong emotions—and it still is for some people, particularly those who feel there is too little of it, or too much, in today's society. However, although a 2005 Gallup poll found that 94 percent of Americans consider themselves at least somewhat patriotic, it is likely that quite a few of them do not feel as deeply emotional about it as was common in the past. Emotions are often rooted in childhood experiences, and for decades now the symbols of patriotism—songs, the Pledge of Allegiance and the American flag—have not been as prominent in the lives of children as they used to be. In many places they are no longer part of the school day, and there are fewer community celebrations than there were before most people lived in cities. The Fourth of July today is marked mainly by fireworks set off or viewed, with little thought about love for America. And so people who have grown up without the heart-stirring feelings formerly evoked by patriotic symbols may treat the subject casually, even when they truly care about their country.

This is not as new a situation as is generally thought. Contrary to common belief, popular devotion to patriotic symbols did not originate in the early years of the nation, much less with the Founding Fathers; it arose during the latter part of the nineteenth century. Before then, flags were largely for military use, to identify ships or proclaim possession of a fort or city, to inspire soldiers, and sometimes to rally political dissenters. The famous original versions of the American flag, such as the one supposedly sewn by Betsy Ross, were not widely used and did not even fly over public buildings. The flag "stayed on the margins of the new republic," writes Woden Teachout in her history *Capture the Flag: A Political History of American Patriotism.* "In the half century following the revolution, it appeared only as a minor symbol."

To be sure, "The Star-Spangled Banner" was written during the War of 1812 and became popular first as a poem and then as a song. The song refers only to the flag of a fort under attack, however, and was not recognized for any official use until 1889; it did not become the national anthem until 1931. It was the surrender of Fort Sumter in 1861, which marked the beginning of the Civil War, that led to the first widespread use of flags by civilians. United in dismay over the lowering of Fort Sumter's flag, people in the North honored the returning soldiers, and those who subsequently formed the Union Army, by displaying flags of their own, their strong pro-Union feeling both expressed and intensified by what had suddenly become a powerful and enduring symbol. Four years of war during which thousands of ordinary citizens fought and died under the flag on American soil enshrined it permanently in the hearts of the nation.

The defeated South saw the flag as a symbol of Northern oppression, so for some time after the war it was viewed as politically sensitive and used sparingly. But as veterans aged and memories of the conflict came to focus more on past heroism and sacrifice than on the polarizing issue of abolishing slavery, it gradually emerged as a unifying symbol for the nation as a whole. This was particularly true because of the many immigrants who came to the United States in the last two decades of the nineteenth century; born under various flags, their children were drawn together by the encouragement of devotion to the American flag in the public schools.

It was in this era that Flag Day was established and the Pledge of Allegiance was written. Flag Day originated in 1885 at a single elementary school and the idea quickly spread; by 1894 it was mandated by several states, and in 1916 was officially established by a presidential proclamation. The Pledge of Allegiance—published in the *Youth's Companion*, the country's foremost children's magazine, as part of a campaign to sell flags—was first said publicly on Columbus Day in 1892 at an elaborate flag ceremony for the opening of the Chicago World's Fair. On the same day it was recited by millions of schoolchildren throughout the nation. It soon became standard, but was not officially adopted by Congress until 1942.

The Pledge of Allegiance has been altered several times. A number of minor wording changes occurred in its early years. Before 1942 it was said not with hand on heart, but with the right arm extended straight out toward the flag; this was changed during World War II because it too closely resembled the Nazi salute. The most recent change was in 1954 when the words "under God" were added, creating a situation that is still highly controversial. Some people believe that these words are an unconstitutional establishment of religion. Courts have ruled that they are not, because they are merely a well-established formality, like the words "in God we trust" on coins and currency. The reason for adding them during the Cold War, however, was to distinguish the principles of the United States from those of the Soviet Union, which was officially atheist; so it can be argued that the words were intended to have a religious meaning.

Promotion of religion is not the only reason why the Pledge of Allegiance is sometimes opposed. Members of some religions believe that it is wrong to swear allegiance to any power other than God, so when the pledge was compulsory in schools, legal challenges were brought on the grounds that this was a violation of the First Amendment's guarantee of religious freedom. Today no one can be forced to say it, but there are still protests by people who feel that for it to be led in classrooms, thus forcing objectors to refuse in front of other children, is de facto coercion. Another argument used against it is that teaching children to say it by rote when they are too young to understand its meaning results in their never taking it seriously. Still another is that Americans' allegiance should be to the Constitution rather than a mere flag. Thus there are many reasons why people who oppose the Pledge of Allegiance cannot be assumed to be unpatriotic.

Nevertheless, a small minority of people are against honoring the American flag, and a few have gone so far as to burn it. Flag burning began in the 1960s and created a furor, especially after the Supreme Court ruled in 1989 that it is a constitutionally protected form of free speech. Several attempts have been made to ban flag burning through a constitutional amendment. Almost no one approves of the practice and many find it highly offensive, yet opponents of the proposed amendment believe that to restrict freedom would be a worse violation of American principles than the degradation of the flag.

During the 2008 presidential campaign, patriotism became a political issue, with candidates accused of being unpatriotic even for trivial reasons such as not wearing a flag pin, something that was rarely worn by anyone prior to the terrorist attacks of September 11, 2001. Among the chief values of patriotism is that in times of trouble it can unite people and give them a sense of belonging to something larger than themselves, yet ironically, in recent years it has been more of a divisive force than a unifying one. There are signs that this is changing and that Americans across the political spectrum are starting to see patriotism in terms of a desire to serve their fellow citizens and to improve the nation.

Notes

1. Mark Twain, "Papers of the Adam Family" in *Letters from the Earth*, published posthumously by Harper & Row, 1962.

CHAPTER 1

What Does It Mean to Be Patriotic?

Overview: There Are Many Differing Opinions About What Constitutes Patriotism

USA Today

USA Today *is a national daily newspaper with the widest print circulation in the United States.*

Ask most American adults today whether they are patriotic, and the answer is a heartfelt yes, regardless of politics.

In fact, 94.5% of Americans think of themselves as at least somewhat patriotic, and 72.2% say they are either very or extremely patriotic, according to a new *USA Today*/CNN/Gallup poll of 1,009 adults. Only 5% of those polled said they were "not especially patriotic."

But exactly what is patriotism?

"In a general way, patriotism means love of country—love of one's country, one's homeland—a very simple emotional attachment to the place where you're from," says Jack Citrin, professor of political science at the University of California at Berkeley.

"After that, agreement tends to dissolve."

Some people religiously salute the flag; some wrap themselves in the flag—literally. Others burn it and say patriotism is about protest.

"There are various ways people love the country, just as there are various ways people love their spouses or love their friends," says Thomas Cushman, a professor of sociology at Wellesley College.

"What Is Patriotism?" *USA Today*, June 29, 2005. Reproduced by permission.

Different Kinds of Patriotism

Patriotism is so complex that academicians have loosely broken it down into categories, although they don't all agree on the labels:

- Devout patriotism. Unconditional loyalty to country. Also called blind patriotism because adherents will support the country no matter what, espousing the ideology, "My country; right or wrong."

- Symbolic patriotism. Attachment to symbols and rituals, such as the flag and patriotic songs.

- Constructive or critical patriotism. Belief that the best way to love one's country is with constructive criticism of the government.

Increasingly these days, disagreement leads to arguments and accusations of others being unpatriotic.

Patriotism "is something that almost everyone thinks is good," says Nolan McCarty, professor of politics and public affairs at Princeton. So if you can attach your idea to something that is good—Mom, apple pie, patriotism—that's a particularly effective way of selling the idea.

"What's newer and more divisive is that people often take it a step further. Not only do they assert that their idea is patriotic, but they discredit other ideas by suggesting those ideas are not in the best interest of the country."

And regardless of where one sits on the political spectrum, that's troubling, says Jacob Needleman, professor of philosophy at San Francisco State University and author of *The American Soul.*

"The whole essence of American patriotism is that you listen to the other side," he says. "There was a time when people disagreed, but it was understood that they were still loyal to the ideas of this country."

That less-divisive view could return if young people turn out to be less polarized than their parents. Students in Douglas Drummond's government and economics class in Omaha, when asked their ideas of patriotism, expressed many different views, but class discussion was fairly calm.

"The kids are pretty open to other people's opinions," Drummond says. "I think they're coming into what it means to be a patriot."

Conflicting Patriotic Traditions Have Served American Values

Woden Teachout

Woden Teachout is a historian and professor of graduate studies at Union Institute & University in Vermont.

The defining image of the flag in our era is the one rising over the rubble of September 11, 2001 [also referred to as 9/11]. On that day, as the emergency vehicles raced through the city and the sirens rose and fell, three men working in the wreckage of Ground Zero found a flagpole in the concrete rubble. A local newspaper photographer caught the moment. The three men stand under the pole with a flag: one man pulling the halyards, one supporting the ropes, one squinting upward ready to lend a hand. Their black helmets and a reflective neon stripe mark them as firefighters; the white dust that covers their trousers and gilds their forearms gives testimony to their work that day. Around them lies a landscape of desolation: a gray background of concrete and steel and a mountain of beams piled in the rubble. The photograph centers on the American flag as it rises slowly from these ruins. The flag holds the memory of chaos: Its presence and the men who raise it are a silent tribute to what happened here. And it stands outside and above that memory. It is a timeless symbol, familiar and classic, a symbol of hope and promise against a background of despair.

In the famous [World War II] Iwo Jima photo of the twentieth century, the pole also rose at an angle, the flag formed the same apex of a rough triangle, and the heroism of ordinary people was exalted: Americans as everyman, working to-

Woden Teachout, "Chapter 8: Flag of Rebirth: Patriotism in the Twenty-First Century," *Capture the Flag: A Political History of American Patriotism*, Basic Books, 2009, 219–223. Reproduced by permission of Perseus Books Group.

gether, raising a beacon of hope above a landscape of destruction. But the firefighters at the Twin Towers are not soldiers; they are civil servants, men whose business it is to save lives. They are not imposing order on a foreign land; they are clearing out a space for order in our own country. They are not planting a flag on new territory, claiming it for the United States; they are raising a flag as a memorial and a gesture of reclaiming. Whereas the Iwo Jima photograph conveys triumph, the photo of Ground Zero evokes a more complex set of emotions: grief, respect, determination, and hope. It is an image of a country united not in war but in rebuilding.

Two Patriotic Traditions

It is tempting to view our two historical patriotic traditions in moral terms and applaud our recent turn toward humanitarianism. Broadly speaking, humanitarian patriotism has been good for our democracy. By emphasizing key values—liberty, egalitarianism, respect for the individual—it established a long political tradition of dissent necessary for returning power to the people. It also inspired many of the moments in which our national circle has been expanded and our liberties granted to a wider group of people. This is the patriotism of the Revolutionary sailors, who saw themselves as practitioners of democracy and the rightful heirs to the civic promise of participation; it is the patriotism of the end of the Civil War, when the Union cause became synonymous with emancipation, and of the civil rights movement, when black Americans were finally able to exercise the voting rights that they had been denied so long. It is the patriotism invoked by [journalist] Bill Moyers, whose flag [pin] drove a wedge between the country and the government, claiming the tradition of dissent amid the drumbeats of war.

Nationalist patriotism, in contrast, conflates a country's ideals and its politics, wrapping both in the flag and making it difficult to separate love of country from support for government policy. The loyalty and faith that nationalists prize facilitate unity but provide little room for the skepticism that the Founding Fathers valued so highly. At their worst, like the Hard Hats [construction workers who rioted in protest against student activists during the Vietnam War] and the Ku Klux Klan in World War I, nationalist patriots exacerbate the worst excesses of democracy. Theirs is the impulse that [French political writer] Alexis de Tocqueville was thinking of when he warned in 1835 against "the tyranny of the majority" in American democracy. It is also the impulse that, despite Moyers's almost lone resistance, defined American patriotism between 2001 and 2008.

But an easy characterization of one form of American patriotism as constructive and another as destructive does not, in fact, hold. Nationalist patriotism also calls us to service, to sacrifice; it calls on our sense of belonging to a larger whole. This was the patriotism that inspired the firefighters and rescue crews of 9/11; it was the patriotism that caused [Vietnam War protestor] Todd Gitlin to hang out the flag of solidarity. For its part, humanitarian patriotism can fail to honor the sacrifice of those who worked to procure the rights we now have. When humanitarians insist on the right to burn the flag, they risk dismissing the real emotions and real sacrifice that coalesce in that symbol. Left-leaning dissidents have learned, to their chagrin, that rejecting patriotism is deeply counterproductive. As Gitlin wrote, looking back on the 1960s: "Many Americans were willing to hear our case against the war, but not to forfeit love of their America." To fight patriotism is to run up against that insurmountable love, while to make the case against war—or for civil liberties or for the extension of rights to others—in terms of patriotism is to invoke the power of that love. Too much nationalism, and patriotism may well devolve into "my country right or wrong," but too much humanitarianism, and sense of community diffuses into the ether—a consequence that invariably ends in conflict.

It is not just the two patriotic traditions that are morally ambiguous; patriotism as a whole is deeply flawed. It is inevitably exclusive. As flags unite, they necessarily divide, and to pledge allegiance to one group is to shut others out of the magic circle. No matter how many times we say "never again," human beings commit atrocities regularly in the name of love of country. And wherever humanitarian forms of patriotism do rise, they are vulnerable to takeover by illiberal nationalist forces. Our own post-9/11 period is a prime example.

A patriotism founded in democratic egalitarianism has the singular ability to cut across lines of geography, race, and class.

A Symbol of Shared Values

Yet patriotism has a productive power that continues to surprise. The swift and overwhelming popularity of the firefighter photograph among Americans of many political beliefs reveals a resonance among Americans that is not always apparent. As often as patriotism has divided our nation, it nonetheless also serves as a shared language among people from very different cultures and political backgrounds, enabling a vast diversity of citizens to draw their personal values from a shared wellspring. There *are* American values, liberty and democracy among them, values that have been enshrined in our founding documents and at key points throughout our history. And even when those values manifest in very different ways, as they inevitably do, they serve as a moral compass. Patriotism provides an ongoing obligation to hold that moral compass; American patriotism, with its tradition of patriotic dissent committed to civil liberties, also provides the means and obligation to correct our path when we find ourselves off course. Because of our history of dissent tied to uncontested common values, we can stray from those values—as we have throughout American history—and still right ourselves in the end. Just as American society found its way back from the repression of World War I, so we can return from the policies of the Bush administration.

To say "I am a patriot" is an act of political engagement. In the United States, it is to acknowledge that we are part of a large and powerful nation—one among others—whose force can be directed for good or for ill. "The cause of America is in a great measure the cause of all mankind," Thomas Paine wrote in 1776. "We have it in our power to begin the world over again." To fly the flag is to stake an active claim to the promise of an American dream that draws its inspiration from the founders and is continuously renewed. It is to seize on the symbol that has always been claimed by ascending groups and to employ its power in service to our common values. A patriotism founded in democratic egalitarianism has the singular ability to cut across lines of geography, race, and class. This patriotism can, with encouragement, create a shared political culture of liberty and justice. In a world as diverse and multifaceted as ours—and as in need of renewal—it is, perhaps, the only thing that can.

The Question of Who Is, or Is Not, Patriotic Often Poisons National Debates

Barack Obama

Barack Obama is the forty-fourth president of the United States. The following viewpoint is a speech that was given while he was campaigning for election.

On a spring morning in April of 1775, a simple band of colonists—farmers and merchants, blacksmiths and printers, men and boys—left their homes and families in Lexington and Concord to take up arms against the tyranny of an empire. The odds against them were long and the risks enormous—for even if they survived the battle, any ultimate failure would bring charges of treason, and death by hanging.

And yet they took that chance. They did so not on behalf of a particular tribe or lineage, but on behalf of a larger idea. The idea of liberty. The idea of God-given, inalienable rights. And with the first shot of that fateful day—a shot heard round the world—the American Revolution, and America's experiment with democracy, began.

Those men of Lexington and Concord were among our first patriots. And at the beginning of a week when we celebrate the birth of our nation, I think it is fitting to pause for a moment and reflect on the meaning of patriotism—theirs, and ours. We do so in part because we are in the midst of war—more than one and a half million of our finest young men and women have now fought in Iraq and Afghanistan; over 60,000 have been wounded, and over 4,600 have been laid to rest. The costs of war have been great, and the debate

Barack Obama, "Remarks of Senator Barack Obama: The America We Love," Speech at a rally in Independence, Missouri, June 30, 2008. www.barackobama.com. Courtesy of Barackobama.com.

surrounding our mission in Iraq has been fierce. It is natural, in light of such sacrifice by so many, to think more deeply about the commitments that bind us to our nation, and to each other.

We reflect on these questions as well because we are in the midst of a presidential election, perhaps the most consequential in generations; a contest that will determine the course of this nation for years, perhaps decades, to come. Not only is it a debate about big issues—health care, jobs, energy, education, and retirement security—but it is also a debate about values. How do we keep ourselves safe and secure while preserving our liberties? How do we restore trust in a government that seems increasingly removed from its people and dominated by special interests? How do we ensure that in an increasingly global economy, the winners maintain allegiance to the less fortunate? And how do we resolve our differences at a time of increasing diversity?

Dissent does not make one unpatriotic, and . . . there is nothing smart or sophisticated about a cynical disregard for America's traditions and institutions.

Patriotism Has Been Questioned for Political Reasoning

Finally, it is worth considering the meaning of patriotism because the question of who is—or is not—a patriot all too often poisons our political debates, in ways that divide us rather than bringing us together. I have come to know this from my own experience on the campaign trail. Throughout my life, I have always taken my deep and abiding love for this country as a given. It was how I was raised; it is what propelled me into public service; it is why I am running for president. And yet, at certain times over the last sixteen months, I have found, for the first time, my patriotism challenged—at times as a result of my own carelessness, more often as a result of the desire by some to score political points and raise fears about who I am and what I stand for.

So let me say this at outset of my remarks. I will never question the patriotism of others in this campaign. And I will not stand idly by when I hear others question mine.

My concerns here aren't simply personal, however. After all, throughout our history, men and women of far greater stature and significance than me have had their patriotism questioned in the midst of momentous debates. Thomas Jefferson was accused by the Federalists of selling out to the French. The anti-Federalists were just as convinced that John Adams was in cahoots with the British and intent on restoring monarchal rule. Likewise, even our wisest presidents have sought to justify questionable policies on the basis of patriotism. Adams' Alien and Sedition Acts, [Abraham] Lincoln's suspension of habeas corpus, [Franklin D.] Roosevelt's internment of Japanese Americans—all were defended as expressions of patriotism, and those who disagreed with their policies were sometimes labeled as unpatriotic.

In other words, the use of patriotism as a political sword or a political shield is as old as the Republic. Still, what is striking about today's patriotism debate is the degree to which it remains rooted in the culture wars of the 1960s—in arguments that go back forty years or more. In the early years of the civil rights movement and opposition to the Vietnam War, defenders of the status quo often accused anybody who questioned the wisdom of government policies of being unpatriotic. Meanwhile, some of those in the so-called counterculture of the sixties reacted not merely by criticizing particular government policies, but by attacking the symbols, and in extreme cases, the very idea, of America itself—by burning flags; by blaming America for all that was wrong with the world; and perhaps most tragically, by failing to honor those veterans coming home from Vietnam, something that remains a national shame to this day.

Most Americans never bought into these simplistic world-views—these caricatures of left and right. Most Americans understood that dissent does not make one unpatriotic, and that there is nothing smart or sophisticated about a cynical disregard for America's traditions and institutions. And yet the anger and turmoil of that period never entirely drained away. All too often our politics still seems trapped in these old, threadbare arguments—a fact most evident during our recent debates about the war in Iraq, when those who opposed administration policy were tagged by some as unpatriotic, and a general providing his best counsel on how to move forward in Iraq was accused of betrayal.

American Ideals Outweigh the Nation's Imperfections

Given the enormous challenges that lie before us, we can no longer afford these sorts of divisions. None of us expect that arguments about patriotism will, or should, vanish entirely; after all, when we argue about patriotism, we are arguing about who we are as a country, and more importantly, who we should be. But surely we can agree that no party or political philosophy has a monopoly on patriotism. And surely we can arrive at a definition of patriotism that, however rough and imperfect, captures the best of America's common spirit.

What would such a definition look like? For me, as for most Americans, patriotism starts as a gut instinct, a loyalty and love for country rooted in my earliest memories. I'm not just talking about the recitations of the Pledge of Allegiance or the Thanksgiving pageants at school or the fireworks on the Fourth of July, as wonderful as those things may be. Rather, I'm referring to the way the American ideal wove its way throughout the lessons my family taught me as a child.

One of my earliest memories is of sitting on my grandfather's shoulders and watching the astronauts come to shore in Hawaii. I remember the cheers and small flags that people waved, and my grandfather explaining how we Americans could do anything we set our minds to do. That's my idea of America.

I remember listening to my grandmother telling stories about her work on a bomber assembly line during World War II. I remember my grandfather handing me his dog tags from his time in [General George S.] Patton's army, and understanding that his defense of this country marked one of his greatest sources of pride. That's my idea of America.

Patriotism is always more than just loyalty to a place on a map or a certain kind of people. Instead, it is also loyalty to America's ideals.

I remember, when living for four years in Indonesia as a child, listening to my mother reading me the first lines of the Declaration of Independence—"We hold these truths to be self-evident, that all men are created equal. That they are endowed by their Creator with certain unalienable rights, that among these are Life, Liberty and the pursuit of Happiness." I remember her explaining how this declaration applied to every American, black and white and brown alike; how those words, and words of the United States Constitution, protected us from the injustices that we witnessed other people suffering during those years abroad. That's my idea of America.

As I got older, that gut instinct—that America is the greatest country on earth—would survive my growing awareness of our nation's imperfections: its ongoing racial strife; the perversion of our political system laid bare during the Watergate hearings; the wrenching poverty of the Mississippi Delta and the hills of Appalachia. Not only because, in my mind, the joys of American life and culture, its vitality, its variety and its freedom, always outweighed its imperfections, but because I learned that what makes America great has never been its perfection but the belief that it can be made better. I came to understand that our revolution was waged for the sake of that belief—that we could be governed by laws, not men; that we could be equal in the eyes of those laws; that we could be free to say what we want and assemble with whomever we want and worship as we please; that we could have the right to pursue our individual dreams but the obligation to help our fellow citizens pursue theirs.

For a young man of mixed race, without firm anchor in any particular community, without even a father's steadying hand, it is this essential American idea—that we are not constrained by the accident of birth but can make of our lives what we will—that has defined my life, just as it has defined the life of so many other Americans.

Patriotism Is Loyalty to the Nation's Ideals

That is why, for me, patriotism is always more than just loyalty to a place on a map or a certain kind of people. Instead, it is also loyalty to America's ideals—ideals for which anyone can sacrifice, or defend, or give their last full measure of devotion. I believe it is this loyalty that allows a country teeming with different races and ethnicities, religions and customs, to come together as one. It is the application of these ideals that separate us from Zimbabwe, where the opposition party and their supporters have been silently hunted, tortured or killed; or Burma, where tens of thousands continue to struggle for basic food and shelter in the wake of a monstrous storm because a military junta fears opening up the country to outsiders; or Iraq, where despite the heroic efforts of our military, and the courage of many ordinary Iraqis, even limited cooperation between various factions remains far too elusive.

I believe those who attack America's flaws without acknowledging the singular greatness of our ideals, and their proven capacity to inspire a better world, do not truly understand America.

Of course, precisely because America isn't perfect, precisely because our ideals constantly demand more from us, patriotism can never be defined as loyalty to any particular leader or government or policy. As Mark Twain, that greatest of American satirists and proud son of Missouri, once wrote, "Patriotism is supporting your country all the time, and your government when it deserves it." We may hope that our leaders and our government stand up for our ideals, and there are many times in our history when that's occurred. But when our laws, our leaders or our government are out of alignment with our ideals, then the dissent of ordinary Americans may prove to be one of the truest expressions of patriotism.

The young preacher from Georgia, Martin Luther King Jr., who led a movement to help America confront our tragic history of racial injustice and live up to the meaning of our creed—he was a patriot. The young soldier who first spoke about the prisoner abuse at Abu Ghraib [a prison in Iraq]—he is a patriot. Recognizing a wrong being committed in this country's name; insisting that we deliver on the promise of our Constitution—these are the acts of patriots, men and women who are defending that which is best in America. And we should never forget that—especially when we disagree with them; especially when they make us uncomfortable with their words.

Beyond a loyalty to America's ideals, beyond a willingness to dissent on behalf of those ideals, I also believe that patriotism must, if it is to mean anything, involve the willingness to sacrifice—to give up something we value on behalf of a larger cause. For those who have fought under the flag of this nation—for the young veterans I meet when I visit Walter Reed [Army Medical Center]; for those like John McCain [the Republican candidate in the 2008 presidential election] who have endured physical torment in service to our country—no further proof of such sacrifice is necessary. And let me also add that no one should ever devalue that service, especially for the sake of a political campaign, and that goes for supporters on both sides.

We must always express our profound gratitude for the service of our men and women in uniform. Period. Indeed, one of the good things to emerge from the current conflict in Iraq has been the widespread recognition that whether you support this war or oppose it, the sacrifice of our troops is always worthy of honor....

Young People Are Ignorant of America's Past

As we begin our fourth century as a nation, it is easy to take the extraordinary nature of America for granted. But it is our responsibility as Americans and as parents to instill that history in our children, both at home and at school. The loss of quality civic education from so many of our classrooms has left too many young Americans without the most basic knowledge of who our forefathers are, or what they did, or the significance of the founding documents that bear their names. Too many children are ignorant of the sheer effort, the risks and sacrifices made by previous generations, to ensure that this country survived war and depression; through the great struggles for civil, and social, and workers' rights.

It is up to us, then, to teach them. It is up to us to teach them that even though we have faced great challenges and made our share of mistakes, we have always been able to come together and make this nation stronger, and more prosperous, and more united, and more just. It is up to us to teach them that America has been a force for good in the world, and that other nations and other people have looked to us as the last, best hope on Earth. It is up to us to teach them that it is good to give back to one's community; that it is honorable to serve in the military; that it is vital to participate in our democracy and make our voices heard.

And it is up to us to teach our children a lesson that those of us in politics too often forget: that patriotism involves not only defending this country against external threat, but also working constantly to make America a better place for future generations. . . .

Our greatest leaders have always understood this. They've defined patriotism with an eye toward posterity. George Washington is rightly revered for his leadership of the Continental Army, but one of his greatest acts of patriotism was his insistence on stepping down after two terms, thereby setting a pattern for those that would follow, reminding future presidents that this is a government of and by and for the people.

Abraham Lincoln did not simply win a war or hold the Union together. In his unwillingness to demonize those against whom he fought; in his refusal to succumb to either the hatred or self-righteousness that war can unleash; in his ultimate insistence that in the aftermath of war the nation would no longer remain half slave and half free; and his trust in the better angels of our nature—he displayed the wisdom and courage that sets a standard for patriotism.

And it was the most famous son of Independence, Harry S. Truman [who lived in Independence, Missouri, prior to and following his presidency], who sat in the White House during his final days in office and said in his Farewell Address: "When Franklin Roosevelt died, I felt there must be a million men better qualified than I, to take up the presidential task. . . . But through all of it, through all the years I have worked here in this room, I have been well aware that I did not really work alone—that you were working with me. No president could ever hope to lead our country, or to sustain the burdens of this office, save the people helped with their support."

In the end, it may be this quality that best describes patriotism in my mind—not just a love of America in the abstract, but a very particular love for, and faith in, the American people. That is why our heart swells with pride at the sight of our flag; why we shed a tear as the lonely notes of "Taps" sound. For we know that the greatness of this country—its victories in war, its enormous wealth, its scientific and cultural achievements—all result from the energy and imagination of the American people; their toil, drive, struggle, restlessness, humor and quiet heroism.

That is the liberty we defend—the liberty of each of us to pursue our own dreams. That is the equality we seek—not an equality of results, but the chance of every single one of us to make it if we try. That is the community we strive to build—one in which we trust in this sometimes messy democracy of ours, one in which we continue to insist that there is nothing we cannot do when we put our mind to it, one in which we see ourselves as part of a larger story, our own fates wrapped up in the fates of those who share allegiance to America's happy and singular creed.

Thank you, God bless you, and may God bless the United States of America.

Patriotism Is More Closely Linked to Dissent than to Conformity

Ron Paul

Ron Paul is a US congressman from Texas. He has run for president twice—in 1988 as the Libertarian nominee and in 2008 as a candidate for the Republican nomination.

For some, patriotism is [as eighteenth-century British author Samuel Johnson famously said] "the last refuge of a scoundrel." For others, it means dissent against a government's abuse of the people's rights.

I have never met a politician in Washington, or any American for that matter, who chose to be called "unpatriotic." Nor have I met anyone who did not believe he wholeheartedly supported our troops wherever they may be.

What I have heard all too frequently from various individuals is sharp accusations that because their political opponents disagree with them on the need for foreign military entanglements, they were "unpatriotic, un-American, evildoers deserving contempt."

The original American patriots were those individuals brave enough to resist with force the oppressive power of King George. I accept the definition of patriotism as that effort to resist oppressive state power. The true patriot is motivated by a sense of responsibility, and out of self-interest—for himself, his family, and the future of his country—to resist government abuse of power. He rejects the notion that patriotism means obedience to the state.

Resistance need not be violent, but the civil disobedience that might be required involves confrontation with the state and invites possible imprisonment.

Ron Paul, "In the Name of Patriotism (Who Are the Patriots?)," Speech Before the US House of Representatives, May 22, 2007. www.house.gov. Courtesy of Ron Paul.

Peaceful nonviolent revolutions against tyranny have been every bit as successful as those involving military confrontation. Mahatma Gandhi and Dr. Martin Luther King Jr. achieved great political successes by practicing nonviolence, yet they themselves suffered physically at the hands of the state.

But whether the resistance against government tyrants is nonviolent or physically violent, the effort to overthrow state oppression qualifies as true patriotism.

True patriotism today has gotten a bad name—at least from the government and the press. Those who now challenge the unconstitutional methods of imposing an income tax on us, or force us to use a monetary system designed to serve the rich at the expense of the poor, are routinely condemned. These American patriots are sadly looked down upon by many. They are never praised as champions of liberty as Gandhi and Martin Luther King Jr. have been.

Liberals, who withhold their taxes as a protest against war, are vilified as well—especially by conservative statists.

Unquestioned loyalty to the state is especially demanded in times of war. Lack of support for a war policy is said to be unpatriotic. Arguments against a particular policy that endorses a war once started are always said to be endangering the troops in the field. This, they blatantly claim, is unpatriotic and all dissent must stop. Yet it is dissent from government policies that defines the true patriot and champion of liberty. . . .

Citizens Accept Loss of Liberty for Fear of Being Called Unpatriotic

Those who mistrust the people and the market for solving problems have no trouble promoting a "war psychology" to justify the expansive role of the state.

This includes the role the federal government plays in our personal lives as well as in all our economic transactions. And certainly the neoconservative belief that we have a moral obligation to spread American values worldwide, through force, justifies the conditions of war in order to rally support at home for the heavy hand of government. It is through this policy, it should surprise no one, that our liberties are undermined, the economy becomes overextended, and our involvement worldwide becomes prohibitive.

Out of fear of being labeled unpatriotic, most citizens become compliant and accept the argument that some loss of liberty is required to fight the war in order to remain safe. This is a bad trade-off in my estimation, especially when done in the name of patriotism.

We must not forget that the true patriot is the one who protests in spite of the consequences, condemnation or ostracism, or even imprisonment that may result.

Loyalty to the state and to autocratic leaders is substituted for true patriotism—that is, a willingness to challenge the state and defend the country, the people, and the culture. The more difficult the times, the stronger the admonition becomes that the leaders be not criticized.

Because the crisis atmosphere of war supports the growth of the state, any problem invites an answer by declaring "war"—even on social and economic issues. This elicits patriotism in support of various government solutions while enhancing the power of the state. Faith in government coercion and a lack of understanding of how free societies operate encourages big government liberals and big government conservatives to manufacture a war psychology to demand political loyalty for domestic policy just as is required in foreign affairs. The long-term cost in dollars spent and liberties lost is neglected as immediate needs are emphasized.

It is for this reason that we have multiple perpetual wars going on simultaneously. Thus the war on drugs, against gun ownership, poverty, illiteracy, and terrorism, as well as our foreign military entanglements, are endless.

All this effort promotes the growth of statism at the expense of liberty. A government designed for a free society should do the opposite: prevent the growth of statism and preserve liberty. Once a war of any sort is declared, the message is sent out not to object or you will be declared unpatriotic. Yet, we must not forget that the true patriot is the one who protests in spite of the consequences, condemnation or ostracism, or even imprisonment that may result. . . .

Whether it's with regard to the defense of welfare spending at home, confiscatory income tax, an immoral monetary system, or support for a war fought under false pretense without a legal declaration, the defenders of liberty and the Constitution are portrayed as unpatriotic while those who support these programs are seen as the patriots. If there's a "war" going on, supporting the state's efforts to win the war is expected at all costs. No dissent! . . .

Civil Liberties Are Being Lost in the Name of Patriotism and Security

Even though every war in which we have been engaged civil liberties have suffered, some have been restored after the war ended, but never completely. This has resulted in a steady erosion of our liberties over the past 200 years. Our government was originally designed to protect our liberties, but it has now instead become the usurper of those liberties.

We currently live in the most difficult of times for guarding against an expanding central government with a steady erosion of our freedoms.

We are continually being reminded that "9/11 [September 11, 2001, terrorist attacks on the United States] has changed everything." Unfortunately, the policy that needed most to be changed—that is our policy of foreign interventionism—has only been expanded. There is no pretense any longer that a policy of humility in foreign affairs, without being the world's policeman and engaging in nation building, is worthy of consideration. We now live in a post 9/11 America where our government is going to make us safe no matter what it takes. We're expected to grin and bear it and adjust to every loss of our liberties in the name of patriotism and security.

The true patriot challenges the state when the state embarks on enhancing its power at the expense of the individual.

Though the majority of Americans initially welcomed this declared effort to make us safe, and were willing to sacrifice for the cause, more and more Americans are now becoming concerned about civil liberties being needlessly and dangerously sacrificed. The problem is that the Iraq war continues to drag on and a real danger of its spreading exists. There's no evidence that a truce will soon be signed in Iraq, or in the war on terror or drugs. Victory is not even definable. If Congress is incapable of declaring an official war, it's impossible to know when it will end. We have been fully forewarned that the world conflict in which we're now engaged will last a long, long time.

The war mentality, and the pervasive fear of an unidentified enemy, allows for a steady erosion of our liberties, and with this our respect for self-reliance and confidence is lost. Just think of the self-sacrifice and the humiliation we go through at the airport screening process on a routine basis. Though there's no scientific evidence of any likelihood of liquids and gels being mixed on an airplane to make a bomb, billions of dollars are wasted throwing away toothpaste and hairspray and searching old women in wheelchairs. . . .

The erosion of our personal liberties started long before 9/11, but 9/11 accelerated the process. There are many things that motivate those who pursue this course—both well-intentioned and malevolent. But it would not happen if the people remained vigilant, understood the importance of individual rights, and were unpersuaded that a need for security justifies the sacrifice of liberty—even if it's just now and then.

The true patriot challenges the state when the state embarks on enhancing its power at the expense of the individual. Without a better understanding and a greater determination to rein in the state, the rights of Americans that resulted from the revolutionary break from the British and the writing of the Constitution, will disappear. . . .

Patriotism is more closely linked to dissent than it is to conformity and a blind desire for safety and security.

Opponents of Government Policies Are Not Unpatriotic or Uncaring

Though welfare and socialism always fails, opponents of them are labeled uncaring. Though opposition to totally unnecessary war should be the only moral position, the rhetoric is twisted to claim that patriots who oppose the war are not "supporting the troops." The cliché "support the troops" is incessantly used as a substitute for the unacceptable notion of "supporting the policy" no matter how flawed it may be. Unsound policy can never help the troops. Keeping the troops out of harm's way and out of wars unrelated to our national security is the only real way of protecting the troops. With this understanding, just who can claim the title of "patriot"?

Before the war in the Middle East spreads and becomes a world conflict, for which we'll be held responsible, or the liberties of all Americans become so suppressed we can no longer resist, much has to be done. Time is short but our course of action should be clear. Resistance to illegal and unconstitutional usurpation of our rights is required. Each of us must choose which course of action we should take—education, conventional political action, or even peaceful civil disobedience, to bring about the necessary changes.

But let it not be said that we did nothing.

Let not those who love the power of the welfare/warfare state label the dissenters of authoritarianism as unpatriotic or uncaring. Patriotism is more closely linked to dissent than it is to conformity and a blind desire for safety and security. Understanding the magnificent rewards of a free society makes us unbashful in its promotion, fully realizing that maximum wealth is created and the greatest chance for peace comes from a society respectful of individual liberty.

Patriotism Is Love of Country, Not of Government or Its Policies

Ron Sparks

Ron Sparks works in information technology and writes a blog called The Binary Biker *about motorcycles, technology, politics, and everything else that interests him.*

Patriotism is defined, by Dictionary.com, as "devoted love, support, and defense of one's country; national loyalty."

That's it; that's all there is to the definition of patriotism. If you'll notice, there is no sub-clause of that definition that states a patriot must support the troops in the exact same fashion as the vocal majority/minority. There is no clause that demands a patriot must be Republican, or any other political party. In fact, the definition says love of country—not of government or policies or leaders or figureheads.

The calls to action within the definition of patriotism are simple; support, love, and defend your country. The greatest truths are often deceivingly simple and elegant—*and are usually worthless as a result*. Just so with the definition of patriotism. It's so simple that there are, literally, millions of possible definitions that can apply to it. And so, it becomes meaningless at any level except the highest.

It's as simple as supporting, loving, and defending my country. And as complex as that.

Because patriotism is such an open-ended and subjective concept, we must, all of us, decide what it means and how to best act upon it. You, me, your coworker, your spouse, your siblings, your friends; we must all decide for ourselves what patriotism really is and how (and if) to act upon it.

Ron Sparks, "Blind Patriotism Is Rampant," Binarybiker.com, March 7, 2010. Reproduced by permission.

Blind Patriotism Is Sweeping the Nation

What do most people do? How do the teeming masses define patriotism? The answer is simple; they choose the path of least resistance and define it the same way everyone around them does. That's a dangerous and troubling realization, people. People don't consciously think about what patriotism is; they blindly follow the lead of the mob they find themselves in.

I've ranted and railed about how the average man or woman on the street displays an astounding lack of critical thinking skills in my blogs. I've agonized over the split between science and religion. I've decried the use of pseudoscience to gain false validity to decidedly nonscientific disciplines. I encourage and feed debate and differing opinions. But I was never called unpatriotic—until just recently.

There is a wave of patriotism devoid of critical thought sweeping this nation. Blind patriotism. It revolves around the United States military and the troops who put their lives on the line. It's all over the social networks and I'm sure you've seen the messages floating around, virally growing and feeding as people blindly agree and forward on to others.

There is no room for discussion about what this means. There is no latitude to define how (or if) you support the troops. You can't comment that you don't support the reasons the government put our young men and women in danger. You either support the troops or you do not. There is no middle ground. That, people, is a False Choice Fallacy.

The false choice is that if you don't support the troops (or at least appear to) exactly the same way as everyone else, you are unpatriotic. I know—because I tried to leverage my critical thinking skills on a patriotic debate on Facebook recently and was labeled unpatriotic. I had the gall to ask the forum for specifics, for clarification, for facts. I had the nerve to break from the herd and speak out. . . .

It Is Not Unpatriotic to Question the Government

People in the thread started pulling out "personal credentials" to impress upon me how firmly entrenched their patriotism is. They had relatives who had fought in three wars. They were married to a soldier. They had served three tours in Iraq or Afghanistan. They passive-aggressively told me they felt sorry for me and they supposed that even someone like me deserves the right to an opinion. It felt very much like a fundamentalist Christian telling me I was going to burn in hell but there was still hope for me if only I would do exactly what they told me to do.

I very calmly informed them that I, too, had "credentials" and that they don't mean much when it comes to defining personal patriotism. I grew up a Navy brat, moving all over the country my entire childhood as my father was stationed in different places. My brother was/is a US Marine. My brother-in-law is a Commander in the Navy. My grandfather on my mom's side fought in the Pacific in WWII [World War II]. My grandfather on my father's side was a POW [prisoner of war] for months in WWII, received the Purple Heart, and was actually *knighted* by the French government for his valor in the Battle of the Bulge. My best friend in the world is currently halfway across the world in Dubai—a Navy diver who holds the extremely dangerous job of looking for mines attached to ships and floating in the harbor. I, personally, spend 40+ hours a week as a consultant for the Army National Guard; I am an IT [information technology] contractor in charge of some very significant software projects with the Guard. I come from a family with a *very* strong military background.

And yet I still ask questions. . . .

It was [African American human rights activist] Malcolm X who said, "You're not supposed to be so blind with patriotism that you can't face reality. Wrong is wrong, no matter who says it." It's wrong to denounce our president for being a diplomat who wants to wage war at the negotiation table instead of in the streets. It's wrong to give up your liberties for the illusion of temporary security. It's wrong to send our troops to die when there may be other options available to us. It's wrong to label someone who questions the government as unpatriotic, since patriotism has nothing to do with government and everything with country.

Do I support my country? Yes—I work, I vote, I debate, and I use my brain to weigh issues and question our government; just as every loyal American should.

Do I love my country? Yes—the United States of America is, in my opinion, the best nation in the world, from sea to shining sea. The United States is a beautiful country, founded on amazing ideals, and has been a shining beacon for the world to follow for generations.

Do I defend my country? Yes—while I can never be a soldier, I do what I can to support our troops by keeping their IT systems working and by making sure our government doesn't cavalierly send them into harm's way.

Do I support our troops? Yes, I do. There are times and reasons why we have to send our troops in harm's way. There are valid reasons in the wars we are fighting today. I do think we're too quick, though, to send the troops in harm's way sometimes.

Ultimately, I think the concept of "nations" is nothing more than "tribalism." I long for the day when borders are no longer necessary and we speak not of nations, but of humanity, but that day is not today. Until then, I choose to support, love, and defend the United States of America in the way I see best.

Just because it's not the same way the mindless masses think doesn't mean I am unpatriotic. I could argue that I am more patriotic than them, because I think about it and have consciously chosen the reasons for my patriotism.

People, don't be blindly patriotic; think about it. Decide why you are patriotic. And above all, *question* everything. As [historian and political activist] Howard Zinn said, "Dissent is the highest form of patriotism."

Patriotism Means Commitment to One's Own Country, Not Just to Universal Ideals

Jack Kerwick

Jack Kerwick is a conservative columnist at several websites and an adjunct instructor of philosophy at Rowan University in New Jersey.

I recently pointed out the ambiguity in which the term "racism" is bathed. Today, I would like to consider two other terms that have played no small role in our political vocabulary, but which are no less ambiguous. They are "patriotism" and "anti-Americanism."

Since I am interested in the former only as it has found expression in the context of America, whatever these terms may mean, they must be treated as opposite sides of the same coin: to be genuinely "anti-American" is to be unpatriotic, for American patriotism consists in *love* for, not animosity toward, America.

An American patriot loves his or her country. I don't believe anyone would take exception to this proposition. But what does it really *mean*?

Doubtless, the vast majority of contemporary Americans to whom this question is posed—and virtually all Republicans and Democrats—will reply that the American patriot is one who has an unwavering commitment to the "principles" or "ideals" of "liberty" and "equality" on which this nation was founded and that are encapsulated in our "national creed," the Declaration of Independence. I find this conception of America—as a society constructed in accordance with ab-

Jack Kerwick, "Reflections on Patriotism and Anti-Americanism," About.com, May 23, 2008. Reproduced by permission.

stract, tradition-neutral propositions—to be self-delusional, but for present purposes that is irrelevant. *American* patriotism must be something other than this.

Just as he loves his relatives and friends no less for their faults . . . so [the American patriot] loves his country no less for its shortcomings.

The "self-evident" and "inalienable rights to Life, Liberty, and the pursuit of Happiness" that are held to express a principle or ideal of equal worth to which American patriots are allegedly devoted are purportedly *universal* in scope. Both the rights themselves as well as the knowledge of them are possessed by all people in all places and at all times. What this means is that, theoretically at least, every human being on the planet could be just as committed to these "principles" of "the American Founding" as Americans themselves. Surely no one would deny that there are *in fact* millions of non-Americans that do indeed profess such commitment. After all, the presumption that third world immigrants share this universalistic vision is what prompts Democrats and Republicans to labor inexhaustibly, attempting to convince the majority of Americans to relax immigration restrictions, and it is the presumption that this vision is what keeps the majority of Arabs and Muslims subscribing to the notion that Republicans, under President George W. Bush, try to elicit support for their "democratizing" efforts throughout the Middle East.

But if to be an American patriot is to embrace principles that are universal in origin and scope, and if non-Americans embrace these very principles, then it follows that *they* are *American* patriots! You see the problem? Love of country, like love of family and love of friends, is a *local*, not a *universal*, affair. The family man is not a man who has sworn to uphold "principles" that *all* "family men" in all places and at all times are equally committed to upholding; the "family man" is the man who exhibits devotion, fidelity, and love to *his* family. It is the tireless *partiality* he shows toward his own family that prompts us to laud him as a family man. Similarly, the American patriot loves his country not because of the universal principles that it supposedly affirms, but because it is *his* country.

Patriots Love Their Country Despite Its Faults

The American patriot knows that his country, not unlike his family and his friends, has faults. But just as he loves his relatives and friends no less for their faults (after all, he is well aware that he has defects of his own), so he loves his country no less for its shortcomings. His country is his home. It is from its history, its institutions, its customs, its laws, and its people that the patriot draws his very identity as the unique person that he is.

The patriot will steadfastly resist evaluating his country in terms of ideal canons of "perfection." A man who spares no occasion to condemn his wife and children because they have failed to satisfy his ideal of perfection is a tyrant, and one who judges his friends as such is ignorant as to what friendship is. Similarly, a man who relentlessly criticizes his country because he believes that it has failed to live up to some utopian ideal by which he is seized loves not his country, but an abstraction that is the product of his imagination, not a being of flesh and blood (so to speak), but a phantom.

This brings us to "anti-Americanism."

There is nothing at all wrong with criticizing one's country, just as there is nothing at all wrong with criticizing one's family, one's friends, or oneself. In fact, love, whether self-directed or other-oriented, must inspire a willingness to be critical, because love is an uncompromising concern for another person's well-being. Only through criticism can we be made aware of our weaknesses and be prompted to overcome, or at least manage them. Some criticism is indispensable to both personal *and* national well-being.

There are two crucial qualifications to keep in mind, however. For criticism to be consistent with love, for it to serve the productive function of helping the beloved to realize its potentialities, it first must be directed toward aspects of the beloved's being, not the beloved itself, and secondly, it must be articulated charitably and episodically, not contemptuously and incessantly.

What distinguishes the anti-American critic from the pro-American critic, the unpatriotic from the patriotic, is that the patriot has a healthy love for his country while the anti-patriot does not.

There are those who criticize America for being conceived in slavery and genocide. They say its very structures are imbued with such abominable evils as racism, sexism, heterosexism, homophobia, and classism. These people must want the concept of American to be *radically* rewritten. They must want to abolish the America that *exists* and favor constructing one that *has never been*. This is not love, or at least not the kind of love to which most people (who aren't suicidal) would want to be subjected. Would we say a man *loves* his wife if he wants to destroy her so she can be transformed into an entirely different person?

The critic who I describe as being "anti-American" could respond by insisting that he really *does* love his country, just as the abusive husband believes—with every fiber of his being—that he loves his wife more than life itself. Perhaps this critic is sincere. I don't pretend to know exactly what love is.

I do know, however, that a love like this is far worse than hate.

Patriotism Is a Complex and Deeply Personal Emotion

Maryna Hrushetska

Maryna Hrushetska is the executive director of the Los Angeles Craft and Folk Art Museum.

Those closest to me are well aware of my great love affair with sleep and morning rituals of green tea and meditation. In general, I rarely make commitments "before the double digits" to preserve my delicate balance, however, this morning I simply could not resist the invitation to attend the Optimist's Breakfast on the topic of—"What does patriotism mean to me?" . . .

On this cold and rainy Friday the 13th [in February 2009], over 100 artists, community leaders, philanthropists, politicians, big thinkers, and a high school class from Topanga, California, gathered to consider the issue of patriotism and munch on bacon & eggs (which were very tasty, btw [by the way]). The first couple of speakers were local politicians (the usual suspects . . .), and despite their clear commitment to local issues and love of Los Angeles, their rather convoluted ramblings on patriotism left me rather unmoved. . . .

Once the artists took the podium, the rather tired and seemingly obligatory pronouncements of "patriotism" by politicians transformed into intense, emotional, and uplifting personal stories of the *process* of becoming patriotic. Perhaps politicians have an inherent disadvantage discussing patriotism since the approved definitions of the term are so narrow. As a daughter of immigrants, I was touched by president of Otis College Samuel Hoi's story of being born in Hong Kong, under foreign rule, which left him with a British passport

Maryna Hrushetska, "Patriotism—Simple Concept or Complex Reality?" CAFAM (Craft and Folk Art Museum), February 13, 2009. www.cafam.org. Reproduced with permission.

with the "Country of Birth" section left blank. This bureau-cratic colonial by-product left a mark on a young mind un-sure of his place in a shifting landscape. Samuel spoke about the gratitude and relief he felt becoming an American citizen, but eloquently shared that his love for his adopted homeland was cemented in the midst of the of September 11, 2001 [ter-rorist attacks on the United States] tragedy.

Like all love affairs, the affection for one's country is fluid and based on mutual respect.

Many Views of Patriotism

The regal air of Tongva tribe sage, cultural activist, and envi-ronmental educator Cindi Alvitre literally transformed the gathering with her powerful, ceremonial greeting declared in her native tongue. Her concept of patriotism had little to do with flag-waving or baseball-playing, but with a primal con-nection to the land. In keeping with her indigenous beliefs and values, patriotism to Cindi translates into honoring and protecting the soil beneath her feet. She boldly declared her loyalty to the land not the sociopolitical system. Her environ-mental view of patriotism seemed to provide the most holistic definition of the question, *how can we claim to love our coun-try while literally destroying its foundation?*

Diverse comments from artists, community leaders, and citizens, some in accented English, some in local dialects, made it clear that patriotism is a beautifully complex and deeply personal emotion not a rote, vacuous declaration made for political gain. Emotional references to the Tiananmen Square massacre [protests in China in 1989 in which hun-dreds of people were killed], civil rights rallies, and several mentions of [First Lady] Michelle Obama's much publicized comment about "being proud of her country for the first time" illustrated that like all love affairs, the affection for one's country is fluid and based on mutual respect.

Merriam-Webster's dictionary simply defines patriotism as love for or devotion to one's country, however, the true meaning is highly dependent on context and philosophy. The classic version of patriotism developed by the Greeks was based on an ethical theory of altruism and benevolence, not on the tribal affiliations often expressed in nationalism. When speaking of moral duty towards others, the issue of application is a tricky one. Does our altruism (or patriotism) extend only to the borders of land, culture, religion, gender, and ethnicity, or does it apply equally to all humans?

My thoughts? Well, Ms. Cosmopolite doesn't carry around a globe for nothing!

[As Spanish musician Pablo Casals wrote,] "The love of one's country is a splendid thing. But why should love stop at the border?"

True Patriotism Demands Commitment to Continuing Progress

Eric Liu and Nick Hanauer

Eric Liu and Nick Hanauer are educators and entrepreneurs who live in Seattle. Together they founded the True Patriot Network to advance the ideals presented in their book The True Patriot, *from which the following viewpoint is excerpted. Liu was a White House speechwriter for President Bill Clinton.*

No nation on Earth has America's greatness of spirit and purpose.

There are other great nations, to be sure: great in scale or power. *But no other nation on Earth is dedicated to a proposition.* No other nation was founded to give people a second chance. No other nation prides itself on being the world's laboratory, demonstrating what happens when you intermingle the peoples of the earth.

Across the span of centuries, America has embodied the very essence of human striving: We have set forth great ideals and have tried to live by them. We have sometimes faltered, sometimes failed. We have always tried again. With each generation, we inch closer to fulfilling our promise. Ever perfectible but never perfect, America is in a constant state of becoming, and this unending progress is our heritage.

But America today is in danger of drifting from its best traditions. We have allowed false prophets of selfishness to obscure our vision. We have grown numb to a creeping cynicism about progress and public life. We crave human connection yet hide behind walls. We worship the money chase yet decry the toll it exacts on us. We allow the market to dominate our

Eric Liu and Nick Hanauer, "Patriotism: A Manifesto," *The True Patriot*, Sasquatch Books, 2007. Reproduced by permission of The True Patriot Network.

lives, relationships, yearnings and aspirations. We indulge in nostalgia and irony and addictive entertainment, then purge from our hearts any true idealism or passion, any notion that being American should mean something more than "everyday low prices" or "every man for himself."

In the midst of this dislocation and disorientation, so many Americans today yearn for higher purpose, for calling— for some assurance that life matters. We wish to believe there is more to our days than is revealed on our screens. Make no mistake: This is a spiritual crisis. And many of us have found spiritual salves in houses of worship. But we are in a social and political crisis as well. And the time has come for a new great awakening, a revival of the creed and the covenant of our civil religion. The time has come to replenish the content of American character and the meaning of American life.

It is time to return to true patriotism.

Patriotism Means Taking Pride in Achievement

What does it mean today to be patriotic? Patriotism means pride. But true patriotism is *earned* pride: It means appreciating not only what is great about our country but also *what it takes* to create and sustain greatness. It means being proud of how we treat each other, how we plan for the future, how we meet challenges and threats. True patriotism celebrates the hard choices needed to create more opportunity for more people, and the values that guide those choices.

False patriots think that wearing little flags on their lapels is the full measure of their patriotic duty.

Unfortunately, in too many quarters patriotism is understood to celebrate might for its own sake, power as its own end. Patriotism has become a cheap brand, a soundtrack and package of graphics signaling complacent conformity: wave your flag, but, don't rock the boat. Patriotism, to many Americans, signifies only empty swagger. It has been wrested by self-satisfied salesmen singing, "You're with us or against us." It has been used to justify dubious acts of war making and lawmaking. It has been stolen to silence dissent.

This crime has a perpetrator and an accomplice. The Far Right has stolen and perverted the idea of patriotism. It has used the flag shamelessly as sword and shield in its narrow partisan campaign for advantage. But the Far Left is culpable as well: of an intolerable passivity, an acquiescence to this brazen theft of patriotism itself. The more the Right uses the flag to proclaim its toughness, to belittle the defenders of the weak, to celebrate winners, the more the Left shrinks from the flag—and in so doing, ratifies the Right's illegitimate claims. But try as they might in this time of war to make patriotism theirs in perpetuity, the jingoists cannot deny what the people know. We, the people, know: that there is more to patriotism than the beating of chests; that he who professes too loudly how strong and unbeatable he is, protests too much; that dissent is as much a measure of patriotism as service is. And our knowledge will prevail.

We, the people, believe it is time for progressives to reclaim patriotism—not to reinvent it but to restore it; to return to a tradition that is more than chauvinism or showboating. It is time to rededicate ourselves to a true American patriotism, a civil religion of purpose that answers our deepest needs and fears in this time of uncertainty. And this patriotism belongs not to party but to country.

It is time to distinguish, with brutal honesty, between false patriots and true American patriots.

True Patriots Are Faithful to America's Values

False patriots think that wearing little flags on their lapels is the full measure of their patriotic duty. True patriots may sometimes wear such flags too but know that acts, not badges, are the true marker of devotion to country. False patriots say that liberty means simply being let alone. True patriots know that liberty is not just the removal of tyranny or encumbrance; it is the cultivation of a freedom worth having—and this requires common endeavor and shared sacrifice. False patriots say that the pursuit of happiness means getting as much for yourself as you can; that accumulating wealth is righteous. True patriots know that the real American dream is to build a legacy that endures: to aspire for your children more than for yourself, and to leave them with truly equal opportunities to live to the fullest of their potential.

False patriots say that diversity and dissent threaten our cohesiveness and comfort our enemies. True patriots know that what frightens our enemies, foreign and domestic, is our capacity for diversity, disagreement and synthesis.

False patriots think that ideology—*their* ideology—is the only pure way, and they champion ideology over the facts of science or common sense. True patriots know that such fundamentalism is fundamentally un-American—and that the strongest streak in the American character is a fierce pragmatism that mistrusts blind ideology of every stripe and insists on finding what really *works*.

False patriots say that we're number one because we're the biggest, the richest and the mightiest. True patriots know that America is number one because of our ethos of hard work, fair play and second chances—and that if we are to remain the world's beacon, we must remain faithful to those values and set a powerful example.

False patriots say that the wealth of the wealthy is proof of their virtue. True patriots know that until we have a level playing field, on which talent can compete fairly against talent, risk can be shared more fairly, and virtue can emerge without regard to inherited benefits and burdens—until this day comes, having money means only having money.

False patriots treat the land, air and water as their personal dominion, to exploit as they please. True patriots know that we are but stewards, and that our obligation to God and posterity should limit our temptations to exploit.

False patriots say they love America but hate the government. True patriots know that government is the physical manifestation of teamwork and mutual obligation in any free, democratic society.

True American patriotism means freedom, with responsibility.

False patriots say that taxes take away the hard-earned money of self-made men. True patriots know that there is no such thing as a self-made man—that every fortune was built upon safe roads, strong backs, clean air, and bright minds developed by the community, through taxes—and that taxes are therefore not just the price we pay for a healthy nation but the gift we make to our own children.

Principles Are the Foundation of Patriotism

True American patriotism means freedom, *with responsibility.*

Opportunity, with personal initiative.

Purpose, through sacrifice and service.

Community above self.

Contribution over consumption.

Stewardship, not exploitation.

Leadership by example.

Pragmatism tied to principle.

A fair shot for all.

These principles form the core of true patriotism, They are pro-progress, pro-truth, pro-trust, pro-fairness, pro-security and pro-peace. They are, if anything, the distilled precepts of every great faith tradition in American life. They are the commandments of our American civic religion. These principles reveal to us that our best life is not to be purchased on credit, ordered on demand, or reaped in a windfall. True American patriotism calls us to be more than what we are now: to be independent in thought; to be tougher, on ourselves first; to be more compassionate, toward strangers as well as family; to hold fast to old-fashioned ideas of honor even when doing so makes us seem naive; and to judge others sternly—but according to their adherence to this code, not by the badges of their status or station.

What we have stated here is a *public* morality. For too long in our politics, morality has been defined as a set of narrow bedroom issues. These issues are real and often raise wrenching private choices. But of far more consequence to the nation is the morality of our public lives, our public choices and our public actions.

At the heart of our public morality is the idea that he who gives generously is most virtuous and morally praiseworthy; that there is no greater citizen than she who sacrifices; and that there is no greater measure of worth than contribution. These are values we can be proud of. After all, there is no moral system or religion on earth where the guiding ethic is "grab more for yourself."

True love of country is giving ourselves to a cause and a purpose larger than ourselves.

Today, however, sacrifice is not shared at all equally. Millions of Americans are working harder than ever, raising the GNP [gross national product] and pumping up productivity—and yet their own wages remain stagnant and their safety net ragged. These Americans are one missed payment away from foreclosure; one ailment away from financial disaster. Tens of thousands of other Americans are risking life and limb in wars around the world. The current [2007] administration has failed utterly to meet these challenges.

Today's Leaders Fail to Inspire Vision

The problem, though, extends beyond an abysmal administration that, eventually, shall pass. Today's leaders—in both parties—fail to challenge us to raise our sights. They do not ask those who have received most to give back in like measure. They do not ask those in the broad middle class to do much more than keep on shopping, or to imagine a vision of citizenship beyond mere consumption. They do not ask us to serve in places where all citizens—rich or poor, of whatever color—are, for a time, equal. They do not honor us that way. They pander. They promise easy solutions with no sacrifice. They prefer, instead, to enshrine selfishness and self-indulgence—and they pretend that patriotism is just self-love writ large.

But to love our country truly means to rise above "I am because I am." It is to recognize that "I am because *we are*." Love of country cannot be a supersized version of individual narcissism. True love of country—of this country—is love of our children, of a creed that promises *them* a better life before it promises us anything, and embraces the sacrifices needed to make that better life. True love of country is giving ourselves to a cause and a purpose larger than ourselves. And that cause is to make liberty worth having, to make the pursuit of happiness deeper than the quest for personal pleasure, and to leave a legacy of progress and possibility.

We will concede that the tenets of true American patriotism are idealistic—in exactly the way that Thomas Paine was when he penned *Common Sense*, or when Thomas Jefferson wrote the Declaration of Independence. Or when Abraham Lincoln spoke of a union that could not, would not, falter. In exactly the way that Theodore Roosevelt demanded that the state protect the public against the concentration of monopolistic wealth. In exactly the way that Franklin [D.] Roosevelt knew that freedom from want and disease is bound inextricably to the procedural freedoms of the Bill of Rights.

Progressive patriotism is our program. Pragmatic idealism is our method. Idealism is not ideology: It is belief in the possibility of progress. It is faith in the next American dream. And it is a faith that sits perfectly well beside pragmatism, for the things we dream of will be made real only by practical action, by a relentless focus on what truly works rather than on reality-denying doctrine or dogma.

And what, really, is the alternative? We can go on for years or even decades living as we do now, going into debt to pay off debts. We can keep pressing the dispenser button for more morphine-like distraction and amusement to numb us. We can keep on plundering the present without regard to the future. We can keep adding layers of makeup on our ugly made-for-TV politics. We can continue allowing a few elites to rig the game in their favor. We can keep worshipping the market and keep imagining ourselves not as citizens but as consumers.

It is time to face the ailments of our society, reckon with the wounds—and see then that to be American still means something great.

But why should we?

Instead, we can return to the practical way of being an American that every generation has known: a way of being that dispenses with fantasy and with orthodoxy and every other form of self-delusion. A way of being that looks squarely at the challenge and asks "What will it take for us to fulfill our promise?" The American way is always to be searching for a better way; to question constantly whether we are living up to our ideals and whether ideology is distorting our vision. At the heart of this is a commitment to a process: a faith that in a land of so many factions, relentlessly fair and pragmatic inquiry will bring us closer to truth.

Greatness Must Be Earned

It is time to face the ailments of our society, reckon with the wounds—and see then that to be American still means something great. Greatness lies not in the impermanent things like fame and power and material abundance. It lies in the integrity of our choices, the veneration of traditional values, the assumption of responsibility and the welcoming of sacrifice. Greatness is found in a society where fair play is not a slogan for fools but is the covenant that binds us together. It is found in the decision to serve someone else before oneself. It is found in the courage to face painful truths about the true costs of our actions and omissions. It is found in the fortitude to defer the many gratifications all around us. It is found in the power to triumph over lethargy and drift. It must be earned, continuously.

Greatness resides in leaders who ask us to be more than what we have been so far. Truly patriotic political leaders do not ask first about party or electoral prospects; they ask first about country. They ask us to do more. They tell us things we may not want to hear, but should.

At this moment, such leaders are few and far between. But ultimately, and blessedly, greatness resides in the heart of every American, for each of us is the heir to a tradition that far outshines the current culture of corruption and disengagement. So it is time now for us all to declare and sustain a new American patriotism: to call out that greatness within each of us, to challenge each other to choose as the first Americans did—with the next generation in mind—and to dream like the best Americans always have—with the next century in mind. It is time to weave our national life back into the tapestry of virtue that made America's past glorious and that can make our future more glorious still.

This is the promise of a new American patriotism. It is a promise we must all keep.

CHAPTER 2

Is Patriotism on the Decline?

Chapter Preface

It is often said that less patriotism exists in America now than existed in the past. Whether this is true is difficult to determine because customs and conditions change over time, and ways of showing patriotism change along with them.

Certainly there is less public display of patriotism than in the era when most towns held parades on holidays, when literal flag-waving and the singing of patriotic songs inspired gatherings, and both adults and children took it for granted that love of country was felt by everyone but traitors. Today's elderly people grew up during World War II, a time when patriotic feelings were not only officially promoted, but were also spontaneously experienced by the great majority of the public because America had been attacked—just as immediately after the terrorist attack of September 11, 2001, the display of such feelings became common again. In both cases, patriotism imparted a feeling of unity, of belonging to something strong and good that could be relied upon in the face of uncertainty. It is not surprising that older generations miss the shared emotion that was meaningful to them in their youth.

But the world today is not the same as it was in the mid twentieth century. The generation that grew up in the 1960s and 1970s was influenced by the Vietnam War, which had far less public support than World War II and led to open, sometimes violent, reactions against the concept of pride in America.

Moreover, in a culture of growing diversity, people have become increasingly reticent about revealing what truly matters to them, especially when it would mean defending orthodox ideas. It can no longer be assumed that one's friends and neighbors will share one's outlook, and to show enthusiasm for tradition is viewed by same as rather unsophisticated.

Thus as columnist Jacquielynn Floyd of the *Dallas Morning News* has written, patriotism ordinarily "is a kind of dusty holiday decoration that gets pulled out of the attic and displayed on the porch for the Fourth of July. It's a topic for kids' essay contests or the old codgers down at the VFW [Veterans of Foreign Wars], not something you talk much about around the office. It's kinda personal, kinda uncool."

Floyd points out that in election years, this changes; people talk about patriotism, bicker over it, when she feels they should be addressing more important issues. To those with strong political opinions, however, the question of patriotism—particularly *other people's* patriotism or lack thereof—*is* important. It has become a divisive issue rather than a unifying one. On one hand, many believe that the loss of Americans' formerly near-unanimous devotion to their country is dangerous, and will lead to weakening its position in the world. On the other hand, others believe that the danger lies in the possibility that patriotism will result in unthinking endorsement of national policies they consider wrong. Some take this position out of deep conviction—but others do so largely because in some circles, it is fashionable to denounce prevailing views.

To those who have loved America throughout their lives and have actively served it, the latter attitude is offensive. In an article posted at USA-Patriotism.com, Bob Weir, a former detective sergeant in the New York City Police Department, comments on people who disparage patriotism without taking any constructive steps to contribute to society: "They gather with friends over cocktails and hors d'oeuvres as they pontificate about the evils of the country that provides their affluent lifestyle. They'll smirk and sneer at those who salute the flag, preferring to view them as jingoists with an aggressive foreign policy mentality. In their rarified world of café latte and whole bran muffins, they could never appreciate the sacrifices made by those who subsisted on K-rations while sacrificing life and limb so their most ardent critics could enjoy the taste of freedom. Instead of applauding their liberators, they engage in accusatory discourse about the immorality of war. Of course, it's easy to be philosophical on a full stomach."

The vast majority of Americans polled consider themselves patriots. But not all of them express their patriotism in the same way. To some, "dissent is the highest form of patriotism," (a statement widely misattributed to Thomas Jefferson although it actually originated in an online comment made by historian Howard Zinn). And although most people would disagree that it is the *highest* form, they do agree that dissent, when part of an effort to improve America rather than merely run it down, is not unpatriotic. The question of whether patriotism is on the decline, therefore, is a matter of interpretation and can have no definitive answer.

Discouragement of Patriotism Leads to the Loss of National Will

Thomas Sowell

Thomas Sowell, a well-known economist and syndicated colum-nist, is a senior fellow at the Hoover Institution, a public policy think tank. He is the author of many books.

The Fourth of July is a patriotic holiday but patriotism has long been viewed with suspicion or disdain by many of the intelligentsia. As far back as 1793, prominent British writer William Godwin called patriotism "high-sounding nonsense."

Internationalism has long been a competitor with patrio-tism, especially among the intelligentsia. [English author] H.G. Wells advocated replacing the idea of duty to one's coun-try with "the idea of cosmopolitan duty."

Perhaps nowhere was patriotism so downplayed or de-plored than among intellectuals in the Western democracies in the two decades after the horrors of the First World War, fought under various nations' banners of patriotism.

In France, after the First World War, the teachers' unions launched a systematic purge of textbooks, in order to promote internationalism and pacifism.

Books that depicted the courage and self-sacrifice of sol-diers who had defended France against the German invaders were called "bellicose" books to be banished from the schools.

Textbook publishers caved in to the power of the teachers' unions, rather than lose a large market for their books. His-tory books were sharply revised to conform to international-ism and pacifism.

Thomas Sowell, "Does Patriotism Matter?" *Creators Syndicate*, July 2008. Reproduced by permission.

The once epic story of the French soldiers' heroic defense against the German invaders at Verdun, despite the massive casualties suffered by the French, was now transformed into a story of horrible suffering by all soldiers at Verdun—French and German alike.

In short, soldiers once depicted as national heroes were now depicted as victims—and just like victims in other nations' armies.

Children were bombarded with stories on the horrors of war. In some schools, children whose fathers had been killed during the war were asked to speak to the class and many of these children—as well as some of their classmates and teachers—broke down in tears.

In Britain, [Prime Minister] Winston Churchill warned that a country "cannot avoid war by dilating upon its horrors." In France, Marshal Philippe Pétain, the victor at Verdun, warned in 1934 that teachers were trying to "raise our sons in ignorance of or in contempt of the fatherland."

But they were voices drowned out by the pacifist and internationalist rhetoric of the 1920s and 1930s.

Did it matter? Does patriotism matter?

France, where pacifism and internationalism were strongest, became a classic example of how much it can matter.

Decline of Patriotism Defeated France in World War II

During the First World War, France fought on against the German invaders for four long years, despite having more of its soldiers killed than all the American soldiers killed in all the wars in the history of the United States, put together.

But during the Second World War, France collapsed after just six weeks of fighting and surrendered to Nazi Germany.

At the bitter moment of defeat the head of the French teachers' union was told, "You are partially responsible for the defeat."

[French President] Charles de Gaulle, [author] François Mauriac, and other Frenchmen blamed a lack of national will or general moral decay, for the sudden and humiliating collapse of France in 1940.

At the outset of the invasion, both German and French generals assessed French military forces as more likely to gain victory, and virtually no one expected France to collapse like a house of cards—except Adolf Hitler, who had studied French society instead of French military forces.

Did patriotism matter? It mattered more than superior French tanks and planes.

Most Americans today are unaware of how much our schools have followed in the footsteps of the French schools of the 1920s and 1930s, or how much our intellectuals have become citizens of the world instead of American patriots.

Our media are busy verbally transforming American combat troops from heroes into victims, just as the French intelligentsia did—with the added twist of calling this "supporting the troops."

Will that matter? Time will tell.

The Cooling of Patriotism Is Real and Extremely Dangerous

Lloyd Marcus

Lloyd Marcus is a singer/songwriter, entertainer, and the author of Confessions of a Black Conservative. *He describes himself as an unhyphenated American rather than an African American.*

I struggled with whether or not to discuss this topic. Our Haitian neighbors are suffering tremendously [from the 2010 earthquake]. I am extremely proud and thank God that we, America, were first on the scene, doing what we always do: come to the rescue of people in need. I questioned, "*Lloyd, are you making much ado about nothing?*" Well, you be the judge.

I am confident that Indianapolis Colts football player Pierre Garçon meant no disrespect to the USA when he waved the *Haitian flag* after the Colts' victory over the Jets in the AFC [American Football Conference] championship game. However, I must confess that it rubbed me the wrong way. Please, this is not a rebuke of the young, excited athlete. He simply wanted to give hope and a shout-out to his homeland. I only wish Garçon had waved both flags: the Haitian flag and Old Glory.

Frankly, I feel that taking pride in being an American simply is not what it used to be. In his 1989 farewell speech, President Ronald Reagan expressed his concern that the kind of patriotism we grew up with was fading away. I call it "patriotism cooling." Reagan said that parents were questioning the necessity to teach their children about the greatness of America and the sacrifices which were made for the freedom and liberty we enjoy. Garçon not even thinking to wave the U.S. flag is testimony of the "patriotism cooling" Reagan saw coming.

Lloyd Marcus, "Dissing America," *American Thinker*, February 11, 2010. Reproduced by permission.

Unlike "global warming," "patriotism cooling" is real and extremely dangerous. In our schools, national pride is considered biased, ignorant, and rude. How dare we think of America as exceptional?! Our kids are no longer taught the incredible sacrifice our boys at Normandy made for freedom. I recently read that educators are pushing a new curriculum which would eliminate much of America's early history. The more ignorant our kids are of the value, the struggle, the uniqueness, and the price of freedom, the more passive they are when freedoms are systematically taken away. And yet, our schools are teaching songs about Barack Hussein Obama, mmm . . . mmm . . . mmm.

The Gradual Decline of Patriotism

Patriotism cooling did not happen overnight. Incrementally, *à la* death by a thousand cuts, America has been dissed by television, Hollywood, schools, Democrats, the Left, and most outrageously, even the president of the United States. Democrat Congressman Jack Murtha accused our military of rape and murder. Democrat Senator Dick Durbin accused America's treatment of GITMO [Guantánamo Bay detention center in Cuba] detainees as being equal to the Nazis' death camps, the Soviet gulags [forced labor camps], and the genocidal campaigns of [leader of Cambodian Communist movement] Pol Pot. President Obama accused the U.S. of arrogance. He chastised us for consuming too much and setting our thermostats too high. Obama travels the world bowing to foreign leaders and apologizing for our country.

Unquestionably, the Left's constant bashing has instilled in some Americans a negative perception of their country. Actor Danny Glover even blamed, believe it or not, the earthquake in Haiti on the U.S. I received the following e-mail from a grandmother who agrees. She wrote, "*. . . we are the ones who are killing the world with our own destructive ways. It just goes to show you we have to change the way we live.*" Hogwash!

Truth be told, America is the greatest, most generous, and most compassionate nation on the planet.

Private citizens gave an estimated $240.92 billion to aid the victims of Hurricane Katrina.

The U.S. has donated billions to Haiti over the years. Thousands of missionary organizations have been attempting to help Haiti for years. Haiti earthquake relief contributions from the U.S. far exceed the contributions of all other countries combined.

A by-product of the Tea Party movement is a resurgence of patriotism. While I am encouraged and grateful, we still have a long way to go. Our children must be taught American exceptionalism. They must be educated about the cost of freedom, which is extremely precious, fragile, and unique to most of the world.

Americans must stop allowing themselves to be intimidated by the Left. Under threat of taking it out on their kids via a lower grade, parents were forced to watch the Al Gore propaganda global warming movie [*An Inconvenient Truth*]. Gore's film is another "cut" to our country. It contributes to the Left's orchestrated, anti-patriotic, "we're the world's bad guys" agenda.

My friends, Lady Liberty deserves much better. Please, stand up for America. Teach your children. I've penned a Haiti relief song titled "Haiti Relief Is Who We Are." Sadly, it is unique because it praises America rather than bashes her. My song celebrates the generosity and greatness of America. It is unfortunate that for these reasons, the song will be considered controversial. Nevertheless, I join with Ronald Reagan in seeing America as it truly is: "a shining city on a hill." I pray you will do the same.

Young People Lack National Spirit

Sally Friedman

Sally Friedman, the wife of a retired New Jersey Superior Court judge, is a longtime contributor to local, regional, and national publications.

I'm not often in public schools these days. Long gone are the years when I was in and out of those buildings as a grade school room mother bearing cupcakes, a library aide during the chaotic middle school years, and a "chaperone"—and yes, that was then the word of choice—for those agonizing high school freshmen dances.

But I was recently back in a high school for reasons too boring and complicated to detail. It could best be described as middle of the road—not an urban school with guards and blown-out windows, not a glitzy suburban palace.

As I watched as the kids trooped in for an assembly program, I tried not to stare at the get-ups, especially not at the new ripped-to-shreds jeans look that must have moms tearing their hair out.

I felt grotesquely old and terribly conspicuous, although only a few of the students even bothered to glimpse at me.

After the attempt to get everyone seated and reasonably quiet, the school's principal signaled for all of us to stand for the singing of the "Star-Spangled Banner."

Most of the kids lumbered to their feet, some almost grudgingly. A few didn't even bother to stand until teachers quickly made their presence felt.

Then the most lackluster singing of that anthem began, with unintelligible words mumbled, and not a single sign of respect or awe or even simple pleasure demonstrated.

Sally Friedman, "Patriotism Gone Sour: Singing of Star Spangled Banner at One N.J. High School Was Appalling," NewJerseyNewsroom.com, May 31, 2010. Reproduced by permission.

I was appalled.

I'd seen this once before, way back in the disillusioned 1970s when kids wore T-shirts with angry slogans and the graduating seniors at our great-nephew's high school walked across the athletic field barefooted and defiant.

That was a long time ago.

But here we are, fighting two wars in distant places, dealing with enormous national and international problems. Foolish me—I thought these were the very times when Americans feel the need for bonding of the patriotic sort.

Later, I asked a teacher whether he thought this was just the Tuesday afternoon doldrums, or whether this was standard behavior. "Oh, most of them don't even know the words and couldn't care less about singing them," was his response.

Sadder still, he seemed resigned to that apathy.

Terrorism—wars—recession—politics as blood sport— and a certain dangerously contagious lack of pride and increasing cynicism—all have diminished our national spirit.

So Much Has Changed

I couldn't help remembering a summer night, decades ago, when my husband and I were traveling home from one of our first and only trips abroad. We had seen Paris, London and Amsterdam. We'd been dazzled by castles and famous museums and charming canals.

But I remember something else even more vividly. I remember how eager we were to be back on American soil after 11 days away from it. On that return trip from London, it felt as if we were flying backwards.

My husband and I couldn't sleep. We could barely even eat back in the days when airlines actually offered food, through that long, long trip.

We wanted to read an American newspaper. We wanted to see the national news. We so longed for home.

As dawn streaked across the sky, and we finally began the descent to Newark airport, somebody in the crowded airplane cabin began cheering. And soon, all of us joined in.

And then an older man a few rows ahead of us began singing "God Bless America," and suddenly, all of us were singing with him. Loud and off-key.

It was corny, it was hokey and it was simply wonderful. There was joy and there was pride in country on that airplane. There was no embarrassment about patriotism. And yes, we all knew the words of that song because we had been singing it all of our lives.

So much has changed since that night when the lights of Newark airport guided our big silver bird to a landing.

Terrorism—wars—recession—politics as blood sport—and a certain dangerously contagious lack of pride and increasing cynicism—all have diminished our national spirit.

Like Chicken Little, we look around and worry that the sky is falling. Nothing feels solid or secure.

And our kids don't bother learning the words to the "Star-Spangled Banner."

My generation, the one that was going to build the Great Society [President Lyndon Johnson's reform program], is bewildered. Where is our common pride of place? Lost in the debris of too much disillusionment, too much disappointment, too little hope?

Looking around that high school auditorium, I wondered whether many of these kids would ever love their country the way their parents and grandparents had.

And sitting there that afternoon, I found myself yearning for the time when every American child would know—and believe—the words "What so proudly we hailed/at the twilight's last gleaming."

And sing them out with pride.

Nearly All Americans See Themselves as Patriotic

Kathy Frankovic

Kathy Frankovic is the director of surveys for CBS News.

Are you patriotic? It's almost the Fourth of July, which makes the question worth asking. But it also is one of those poll questions—like did you vote or have you paid your taxes—where saying "no" can be construed as an admission of guilt. Nearly all Americans see themselves as patriotic, but many have some doubts about the rest of the country.

So are Americans patriotic? Absolutely! Last summer [2006], on the eve of the fifth anniversary of the September 11, 2001, terrorist attacks [also referred to as 9/11], 62 percent of Americans in a CBS News/*New York Times* poll described themselves as "very patriotic." Another 33 percent said they were somewhat patriotic. That left only 5 percent who admitted to anything less.

Threats, wars and crises make the public more willing to "rally round" the president and the country, so it's no surprise that the 9/11 attacks increased the "very patriotic" group. The percentage was as high as 72 percent just after the attacks. In a CBS News/*New York Times* poll conducted ten years before that, it was 55 percent, significantly lower than in 2001, and lower than in the most recent poll.

Although pretty much everyone claims to be patriotic, there are differences. According to last year's poll, patriotism increases with age, and was higher in the Midwest and South than in the Northeast and West. By self-report, Republicans are more patriotic—last year, 76 percent of them said they

Kathy Frankovic, "Nearly All Americans Say They're Patriotic, but They're Not Sure About Everyone Else," CBSNews.com, June 27, 2007. Reproduced by permission.

were very patriotic, compared with 53 percent of Democrats. Self-described conservatives were 24 points more likely than liberals to describe themselves that way.

Conservatives were more likely than liberals to see differences in patriotism between the two groups. A quarter of conservatives believed liberals were less patriotic than they themselves were, a percentage nearly four times as large as the percentage of liberals who felt conservatives were less patriotic.

Personally, Americans may feel more patriotic, but more than half think the average American today isn't.

According to the Roper Center iPoll database at the University of Connecticut, pollsters have rarely asked Americans whether specific candidates or individuals were patriotic. But when they do, Republicans have the upper hand. In early 2004, according to a Gallup/CNN/*USA Today* poll, more Americans said being patriotic applied more to Republican George W. Bush than to Democrat John Kerry. In 1988, more voters thought the current president's father George Bush was very patriotic than thought Democrat Michael Dukakis was. Twenty years ago, in the middle of the Iran-Contra scandal, 73 percent of Americans agreed that [Marine Corps officer and author] Oliver North was a "real patriot."

But there has also been skepticism about politicians using patriotism for political reasons—two-thirds of the public in one long-ago poll said most elected officials and candidates who talk about their patriotism do it as a way of winning votes, not because they mean it.

This skepticism extends to the country as a whole. Personally, Americans may feel more patriotic, but more than half think the average American today isn't.

What Patriotism Means to Americans

But what does patriotism mean? A long time ago, the *New York Times* asked Americans what it meant to be patriotic and whether someone had to do anything to be patriotic. Most said a person didn't have to actually do anything—loving one's country was enough. But there are some patriotic acts. More than six in ten adults in 1983 said serving on a jury or serving in the armed forces was a patriotic act—but even more described voting that way! Easy things to do were seen as patriotic by more people than things that took more time and commitment. So while 77 percent said singing the "Star-Spangled Banner" was a sign of patriotism, only 55 percent said joining the Peace Corps was.

Being patriotic doesn't mean you can't complain. Overwhelming majorities say people who criticize the government or protest against the Iraq war can still be patriotic. People can even complain about taxes (as long as they don't cheat on them). But when it came to voting for a Communist there's a different answer: as European communism was failing in 1989, 73 percent told a *Parents* magazine-sponsored poll that voting for a Communist candidate would be unpatriotic!

Finally, some tactics billed as patriotic may go too far, according to the public. In March 2003, 66 percent of those interviewed in a Gallup/CNN/*USA Today* poll said that changing the name of French fries to "freedom fries" [as was done by some restaurants in 2003 to express anger at France for not supporting the invasion of Iraq] was a "silly idea," not a "sincere expression of patriotism."

Happy Fourth of July!

Patriotism Is Evident Throughout America

Scott T. Sturkol

Scott T. Sturkol is a US Air Force technical sergeant serving in Air Mobility Command Public Affairs.

Every place I live I try to make sure I have an American flag, with no rips or tears, properly displayed in the front of my home. It's not because I'm overly patriotic, it's because I'm so thankful that I live in the United States and that I have the privilege of serving as an Air Force Airman.

The flag in front of my home will fly on Sept. 11, also known as Patriot Day. To me, Patriot Day takes a special place in my life. Since the fateful day of Sept. 11, 2001, my life, like those of many Americans, took on a new meaning after terrorists hijacked four civilian planes and attacked the World Trade Center in New York City with two planes and the Pentagon in Washington, D.C., with one. The fourth plane crashed in a field in Pennsylvania.

I still remember being angered so by the devastation and wanted retaliation for those responsible. What followed in the days afterward, however, was a spike in patriotism across our nation that hadn't been seen in awhile. People were holding the Stars and Stripes closer to their hearts. I was among those people, living among patriots.

The congressional bill to make Sept. 11th a holiday was introduced in the U.S. House of Representatives on Oct. 25, 2001, with 22 co-sponsors. Among them, 11 were Democrats and 11 were Republicans. It passed the House by a vote of 407-0 and passed the Senate unanimously on Nov. 30, 2001. It was signed into law by President George W. Bush on Dec. 18, 2001, creating Patriot Day.

Scott T. Sturkol, "Living Among Patriots," U.S. Air Force, September 11, 2009. www.af.mil. Courtesy of Air Mobility Command.

So why should this be important to all of us? Well for me it's not just about just the military veterans who have died protecting our freedoms since that day and before, it's about all Americans. Each American, I believe deep down, loves this country to his or her core. I believe each American is a patriot.

Patriotism Can Be Seen Everywhere

I see patriotism wherever I go in the military both at home station and abroad. For example on my last two deployments—one to Southwest Asia and the other to Uzbekistan, I recall aircrews taking American flags with them on combat missions to include air refueling and airdrop missions. It's a practice that continues today.

When these service members bring those flags home after deployment, they give them to the special "patriots" in their lives. I had flags I purchased and sent on such missions, and I gave them to my parents, my children's schools and most importantly to my wife. Why? Because I know it's not just me, it's also all the people in my life who work to protect our freedoms. It's the whole patriotic team.

I see the patriotism away from the military, too. I see it when I visit my hometown, especially during Independence Day activities every July 4. Leading every parade is a color guard, which I've even marched in myself, that carries the Stars and Stripes front and center.

And even when it's not Independence Day, I see the patriotism in towns across the land with flags flying high in front of schools, businesses, government buildings, and of course many homes. It's a real inspiration every time I see a flag in the front of someone's home. It tells me immediately they are patriots.

I also see strong patriotism in my own family. My children and grandchildren inspire me every day with their beautiful support and belief in what the United States stands for. My parents, who raised me to believe that what we have in America is something special, as well as my brothers, sister, in-laws and more are also all tried-and-true patriots.

Most importantly for me, one of the biggest patriots I know is my wife. For the nearly 18 years that I've known her, I've never met anyone who can provide the support, love and care of someone like me, a military member, more. She is the one patriot I'm most proud to be associated with for the rest of my life.

My list of fellow patriots goes on and on. The big thing I would like you to remember is that we all have patriots around us and this Sept. 11, remember that you are a patriot, too.

American Patriotism Is Alive and Well

Jeanette Krebs

Jeanette Krebs is the editorial page editor for The Patriot-News, *a newsweekly published in Harrisburg, Pennsylvania.*

Patriot.

It is a great word, full of history and love for our country, that conjures up all sorts of images of flags, fireworks and freedom.

In recent years, however, the term has lost its luster. It's been overused and misused, misplaced and distrusted. Too often it has been hijacked by the Far Right and abandoned by the Left.

The definition of a patriot states it "is one who loves and loyally or zealously supports one's own country."

Most Americans, from all walks of life, would agree to feeling that way, especially in early July while celebrating our nation's independence to the strains of the national anthem.

But that is not the only time.

Our patriotic pulse quickens when we watch American athletes compete. Or when soldiers who are willing to sacrifice their lives for our freedoms are rightfully recognized. Or in moments when our nation pulls together in the wake of a national crisis or disaster such as occurred with the Sept. 11, 2001, terrorist attacks.

Proud Americans, of course, do not walk around in red, white and blue garb on a regular basis to express their patriotism outwardly. Most people keep private the feelings that being a patriot stirs in them, deep inside. Their love for America is as personal as their religion, their family and their politics.

It is sad in many ways that instead of seeing the word [patriotism] as one that unites us, it has come to divide us.

But given that some believe they can measure who is and who is not patriotic, the term has become a loaded label. Does being a patriot still arouse thoughts of stewardship, shared sacrifice and service or ignite anger, frustration and finger-pointing?

All Pennsylvanians should feel a particular affinity with the term, given our state's history with the original patriots, and not allow it to become some hackneyed expression that identifies and separates "us" from "them."

It is sad in many ways that instead of seeing the word as one that unites us, it has come to divide us. There is a sense that you have to join a certain club, take a certain pledge and lean a certain way politically before you can call yourself a patriot.

We see it more and more on the campaign trail, too, especially on the national scene. Each political party tries to corner the market on patriotism while claiming the other is nothing more than a group of thugs trying to destroy our way of life.

Political Views Should Not Be a Factor in Patriotism

There should be no judgment attached to being a patriot.

It doesn't matter what is on anyone's voter registration card or whether they support or oppose health care reform. Whether they rally against "big government" or support our president is not a factor either.

We should take back this precious word for everyone.

It is a strong and affirming term. It's the kind of word that this newspaper's founders first decided they wanted to sit on top of each day's front page more than a hundred years ago.

Americans should not be afraid to embrace their patriotism and know that others with political, educational and philosophical differences from our own are just as patriotic.

We all should be able to feel blessed by what those patriots did to create our independence more than 200 years ago. They helped build a unique nation where patriots can come in all sizes and shapes.

Times are tough—that much we agree on.

Whatever it is that has us frustrated with our government and with one another, we need to bridge the gap. We need to find a way to stick together.

And whether we find our heroes in the past or the present, in George Washington or Barack Obama, patriotism remains alive and well in the United States.

The only mistake lies in thinking otherwise.

A New Form of Patriotism Is Inspiring Americans to Help Each Other

Patricia J. Williams

Patricia J. Williams is a professor of law at Columbia University and a columnist for the Nation.

If the Stars and Stripes are the truest symbol of national pride, then patriotism seems to be flying high. You can feel it as much as see it. At coffee bars in Seattle, in Midwestern farm communities, on college campuses, in New York City subways, Americans from all walks of life—old, young, white, black, Republican and Democratic—are fervently, happily, waving the flag, both literally and figuratively, and bursting with a renewed spirit that is helping redefine what it means to be a patriot. It's a zeal that celebrates more than just symbols: These days Americans are rallying to make citizenship a participatory sport.

It is a welcome shift in mood. After years during which the flag—indeed patriotism itself—has been used as a polarizing line in the political sand, the country seems to have entered an era of energetic involvement in our collective fate. Fueled in part by President Barack Obama's resonant and reiterated call to service, the melting pot of our citizenry is rethinking the matter of our social contract—seeing in it a vehicle for cooperation, a link that allows us to combine our human capital and reinforce the strengths we have in common.

Volunteerism at food banks has risen. Donations to blood banks are up. And interest in national service jobs has skyrocketed: Between November 2008 and May 2009, applications to the AmeriCorps program soared 226 percent over the same period a year before.

No doubt the urgency of these recessionary times has played a role. But it's probably too easy to cast the sudden attraction to the public sphere as merely one big desperate job hunt in a tough economy. "People are looking for something of meaning beyond themselves," notes Marc Freedman, founder and CEO of Civic Ventures and author of *Encore: Finding Work That Matters in the Second Half of Life* (Public Affairs, 2007). Especially among those 50 and older, "there's a practical idealism at work—a desire to leave the world better off than we found it, but a recognition that we're not going to live forever, so we'd better make an impact now."

For too long, patriotism has connoted an unfortunate jockeying about who best loves liberty.

Making a Difference

This yearning to make a difference is perhaps why Thomas Weller, a 61-year-old mechanic near San Diego, patrols the local highways in his station wagon, helping people stranded on the road, then slips them a card that reads: "Assisting you has been my pleasure." Or why Mary Kay Gehring, 52, a former Portland, Oregon, chef, spends hours each week teaching struggling young women how to cook nutritiously for their families. "We're not talking about their drug use," she says. "We're talking about the carrots." Or why in January an estimated one million volunteers showed up at 13,000 projects across the country for the annual Martin Luther King Jr. Day of Service—the largest turnout ever.

Public officials are taking the cues: Last spring, with the enthusiastic urging of AARP [American Association of Retired Persons] and scores of other volunteer organizations, Congress passed, and President Obama signed, the Edward M. Kennedy Serve America Act, a $5.7 billion bill that significantly expands volunteer opportunities for Americans of all ages and helps nonprofit groups marshal and manage the thousands eager to do the work—from feeding the hungry and helping students achieve, to rebuilding cities and greening our communities. Though named for its major sponsor, the bill was a bipartisan coup, a fact marked most dramatically by the intriguing and patient collaboration between Senator Ted Kennedy, a Democrat from Massachusetts, and his friend and frequent ideological foe, Senator Orrin Hatch, a Republican from Utah and coauthor of the bill.

Rarely in our history have people rallied so cohesively across partisan lines to try to make such good things happen. Hatch himself called the achievement a milestone—a nod to "a keystone of our country's traditions" and a big stride toward "renewing the can-do spirit" that in many ways is the essence of true patriotism.

He's got it right: For too long, patriotism has connoted an unfortunate jockeying about who best loves liberty. But we seem to be wearying of this aimless enervation of national spirit. Perhaps it was the accumulated grief of September 11 [2001 terrorist attacks on the United States], or the terrible incentive of Hurricane Katrina's devastation [to the Gulf Coast in 2005], or the debacle of Wall Street. In times such as these, when jobs, homes, and hopes are sliding away, it is hard to ignore our interdependence. If ever there was a time to band together and be inspired by do-gooders like Weller and Gehring, or start a neighborhood watch, or a barter exchange, or a modern-day bucket brigade, now is that moment.

Polls show that a majority of us subscribe to some version of charitable or volunteer service. And studies show that involvement makes us happier. It even seems to be correlated with a longer life span.

Small Contributions

But where to begin and how to squeeze it in? The good news is that no one has to do it all. We tend to imagine that service means we can make "a world of difference" all by ourselves, or that it must be some soaring moment of visible and immediate transformation. This is a punishing standard, and a paralyzing one, unless we leaven our ideals with humility and a sense of proportion. Service can indeed mean putting one's life on the line in the military or giving over one's career to fostering children. But it also includes smaller but no less valuable contributions. It includes the man who stops smoking, stashes away a dollar every time he has a hankering for a cigarette, and gives the money to cancer research. It includes the woman who uses her backyard to teach children how to grow lettuce, the neighbors who socialize on Saturday morning by picking up litter in their local park, the college students who spend spring break hanging dry wall in New Orleans, the bored middle schooler who gets a spark of satisfaction working at the local food bank.

There's a lovely children's tale about a wanderer who comes to a town where all the inhabitants cry out that they are starving. The wanderer proclaims that stone soup is just the thing. To the wonderment of the townsfolk, he sets a large pot in the middle of the square, fills it with water, and places a stone in the pot. Then he instructs the people to go back to their homes and bring whatever they can to flavor the stone. This one brings a carrot; another, a potato; someone else, a turnip—and before long there is a bubbling stew sufficient to feed all.

We Americans have all the ingredients for a magnificent stone soup. But like Kay MacVey, 83, who with her Ames, Iowa, friends has clipped more than $1 million in coupons to ease the PX grocery bills of military families overseas, even more of us must come to the public square with the offering of our choice in hand—some small contribution to toss into what we have just begun to appreciate is a rather magical, all-encompassing pot.

Political Liberals as Well as Conservatives Are Now Promoting Patriotism

Michael Kazin

Michael Kazin teaches history at Georgetown University. He is the author of A Godly Hero: The Life of William Jennings Bryan.

Barack Obama's rise to power has, to many people's surprise, once again made patriotism a liberal faith. At the pre-inaugural concert at the Lincoln Memorial, "This Land Is Your Land," lustily rendered by Pete Seeger and Bruce Springsteen, shared equal billing with "The Star-Spangled Banner." In his inaugural address, the new president evoked "obscure" Americans who "toiled in sweatshops" or "endured the lash of the whip and plowed the hard earth" as exemplary citizens, while denouncing those who "seek only the pleasures of riches and fame." Before him stretched a crowd of some 1.8 million admirers; many, to paraphrase [First Lady] Michelle Obama's controversial words from last winter, were surely as proud of their country as they had been in many years. That throng on the Mall was probably the largest pro-government demonstration in U.S. history. That spirit is probably strong enough to withstand the news that some high-placed Obama appointees had failed to pay their taxes—and may even be bolstered by the president's apology for "screwing up" the process.

The revival of Americanism on the Left is as unexpected as was Obama's victory itself. Since liberals turned against the war in Vietnam 40 years ago, they have struggled to prove that they love their country even while opposing most of the policies of its government. Some abandoned the effort altogether,

Michael Kazin, "A Liberal Revival of Americanism," *Washington Post*, February 8, 2009. Reproduced by permission of the author.

preferring to don a fresh identity as global citizens. The philosopher Martha Nussbaum argued in 1994 that patriotism is "morally dangerous" because it encourages Americans to focus narrowly on their own concerns and to minimize or disregard those of people in other lands. Meanwhile, conservatives led by Ronald Reagan defined patriotism as the need to stand tall against one's enemies and equated liberty with low taxes and a lightly regulated market. From the invasion of Cambodia to the invasion of Iraq, war protesters pleaded, "Peace Is Patriotic," but few on either side paid them much attention.

Liberals Are Adopting Americanism

Then, quite unintentionally, George W. Bush convinced liberals that they should stand up for their own version of the national creed. They condemned his 2000 election as a betrayal of democracy, achieved only after he lost the popular vote and got an assist from a Right-leaning Supreme Court. As the "war on terror" heated up after the Sept. 11, 2001, attacks, liberals accused the president of violating the Constitution by snooping into library and phone records and unapologetically using torture. Then the bloody debacle in Iraq drove many a progressive to dust off the advice of President John Quincy Adams that the United States should not go "abroad in search of monsters to destroy" because "she would be no longer the ruler of her own spirit."

Gradually, a liberal movement flourished, vowing to "take our country back." Activists made it clear they supported the troops in Iraq and criticized only the policy makers who had sent them there to find doomsday weapons that did not exist. Markos Moulitsas Zúñiga, the creator of Daily Kos, the movement's most influential website, is himself a proud Gulf War veteran who thanks the military for giving him "a sense of duty to my fellow Americans." "Those who wore combat boots," he writes, "looked out for each other and took responsibility for them." When such Bush defenders as [radio host]

Rush Limbaugh accused liberals of running the country down, the liberals would now return the charge—with vigor.

That confident tone ran through Obama's coming-out speech at the 2004 Democratic Convention. "Alongside our famous individualism, there's another ingredient in the American saga, a belief that we're all connected as one people," asserted the young state senator from Illinois. That belief applied to "a child on the South Side of Chicago who can't read," he continued, to "a senior citizen somewhere who can't pay for their prescription drugs," to "an Arab American family being rounded up without benefit of an attorney or due process." His speech reminded listeners that compassion for the underdog was also a traditional American value.

During his presidential campaign, Obama went on to blend two of the most powerful and uplifting narratives in U.S. history into a single liberal vision, even though he did not embrace the dreaded L-word. Obama drew on his father's background and his own African name to illustrate the opportunities available to immigrants willing to work hard to realize their own version of the American dream. And he evoked the long crusade for black freedom to demonstrate that "there is no obstacle that can stand in the way of millions of voices calling for change." Taken together, these stories suggested that the real America had always been a multicultural nation, filled with people struggling to put transcendent ideals into everyday practice.

In so doing, Obama built a movement behind his candidacy with praise for past grassroots efforts that similarly sought to "let America be America again," as the poet Langston Hughes famously put it. Obama, the erstwhile community organizer, described such movements as the democratic soul of the nation. "'Yes we can,'" he declared after losing the New Hampshire primary, "was the call of workers who organized, women who reached for the ballot . . . and a king who took us to the mountaintop and pointed the way to the promised land."

Liberals Promoted Americanism in the 1930s

In daubing Americanism with a tolerant, energetically populist hue, Obama and the liberals who flocked to his campaign were echoing their counterparts in the 1930s, an era whose economic hardships have made it relevant again. During the presidency of Franklin D. Roosevelt, the federal government hired artists to paint historical murals in post offices that highlighted the exploits of farmers and workers. The Works Progress Administration published guides to every big city and region, revealing the richness of local histories and cultures. In the new National Archives building next to the Mall, the republic's founding documents were displayed as if they were the relics of secular saints. Meanwhile, filmmakers such as Frank Capra depicted America as one big, friendly house for ordinary people of all religions and races (even if, in the era of Jim Crow [segregation of blacks] the latter had to stay in their own rooms).

Something has definitely changed in the politics of patriotism.

Left-wing movements allied with the New Deal trumpeted their patriotism as well. Labor organizers labeled their cause a fight for "industrial democracy" against "Tory" [extremely conservative] employers. Striking auto workers outside a Ford plant lambasted "King Henry V-8," and a picketer dressed up as Lincoln carried a sign reading, "I Fought for Union Too." In the late 1930s, pro-Soviet radicals even proclaimed that communism was "20th-century Americanism."

Woody Guthrie, a sometime columnist for the *Daily Worker* [a Communist newspaper], wrote "This Land Is Your Land" to make the case that his beloved country ought to be governed for the benefit of its least fortunate people. One verse, routinely omitted when "This Land" is performed in elementary schools, expressed the anger of many Americans who had lost their jobs during the Great Depression: "In the squares of the city—In the shadow of the steeple/Near the relief office—I see my people/And some are grumblin', and some are wonderin'/If this land's still made for you and me." Surprisingly, the 89-year-old Seeger—Guthrie's old friend and comrade—rasped out a variant of those lines when he and Springsteen appeared on the frigid steps of the Lincoln Memorial. To my knowledge, no prominent conservative lodged a protest. If a former Communist can get away with singing a verse frequently considered too radical for schoolchildren at an event to honor a popular new president, something has definitely changed in the politics of patriotism.

Obama often says that he wants to move beyond the "stale debates" that, since the 1960s, have frequently made people who care about politics into bitter opponents. Arguments about who really loves their country are part of what he means, as are skirmishes over race, religion and sexuality.

After decades in denial, progressives have finally realized that they cannot lead America if America does not hold a privileged place in their hearts.

But if Obama believes one can enforce a truce in the long battle over how to apply the founding ideals of the nation, he will be disappointed. Since the 1790s, when Vice President Thomas Jefferson accused President John Adams of betraying the republic's "true principles" with his Alien and Sedition Acts, this conflict has been a vital matter in our politics.

No one competing for national office can afford to be on the wrong side of Americanism, an immensely attractive and remarkably supple creed.

Liberals are still getting comfortable with thinking of themselves as the upholders of civic virtue. And conservatives will certainly try their best to recapture that image, as last fall's attacks on Obama as a European-style socialist demonstrated. But after decades in denial, progressives have finally realized that they cannot lead America if America does not hold a privileged place in their hearts. If Obama is as successful at running the country as he has been at recrafting the national story, his most fervent supporters might come to believe that a majority of their fellow citizens are also proud of them.

CHAPTER 3

Is Patriotism Desirable?

Chapter Preface

Is patriotism a good thing? It would not occur to most people to ask such a question, for patriotism has traditionally been considered admirable. In fact, although the vast majority of Americans say they are patriotic, observers suspect that some do so just because they assume that is the "right" answer or are embarrassed to admit that they have no strong emotions about it.

In universities there has been a growing tendency to disapprove of patriotism, particularly since the 1960s when a strong feeling against the Vietnam War arose. On some campuses it has become unfashionable to favor patriotism, either because of issues it involves or because it is considered "uncool."

In most cases, those who admire patriotism and those who frown on it are talking about two different concepts. Opponents deplore the "My country, right or wrong" attitude they believe patriotism implies, but in reality few patriots have such an attitude; on the contrary, the average American is quick to criticize the government, although patriots do love their country, as distinguished from the government, even when they think specific policies are wrong. Furthermore, patriots rarely feel that the *people* of America are better than people elsewhere—another claim that is often made by opponents—even when they believe that its form of government is better than forms that allow citizens less freedom.

People who deplore patriotism sometimes jump to the conclusion that Americans who call themselves patriots support anything the government decides and are unwilling to tolerate dissent, perhaps because a vocal minority does express such feelings. Yet it should be obvious that this is not true of the majority, for after all, those who serve in Congress are presumably patriotic, and yet whichever party is in power, the opposing party in Congress dissents vociferously. For Congress to agree on national policies is the exception rather than the rule, and for it to overwhelmingly support the president's proposals is also unusual. Moreover, election campaigning consists almost entirely of loud criticism of what is being done by the incumbents. So a good deal of anti-patriotism amounts to attacking a straw man.

Some people oppose patriotism as a matter of principle, even though they are aware it does not necessarily mean blind support for what the government does. They believe that there is danger of the public being led through patriotism to support government policy unthinkingly, which has happened under totalitarian regimes throughout history. Moreover, they see no need for an emotional devotion to a particular nation. It would be better, they say, for people to consider themselves citizens of the whole world. People today do have a feeling of belonging to Earth as a whole now that is has been seen from space as an indivisible and perhaps fragile planet, and if someday there were to be contact with other inhabited planets, there is no doubt about where the public's loyalty would lie. But advocates of patriotism believe that for the present, a more local attachment is indispensable for unity and commitment to values that are held in common.

As Conor Friedersdorf wrote in the web magazine the *American Scene*,

> If loving the United States of America means admiring, upholding and defending the values found in the Declaration of Independence and the Constitution, patriotism is a good thing indeed, even if that intellectually driven love is bolstered by an emotional attachment to our community, our friends and our culture. That is my feeling, and I therefore consider myself a patriot. But if loving the United States of America is severed from admiring, upholding and defending those values—if America is supposed to be some ill-defined thing, and I am supposed to lend my support to whatever the person elected as its president decides—then patriotism is better guarded against than embraced.

Patriotism Fuels and Advances the Nation

Geoffrey Whitener

As of 2010 Geoffrey Whitener was a student at Kealakehe High School, in Kailua-Kona, Hawaii. His essay was one of the top ten winners in a contest sponsored by the Bill of Rights Institute in Arlington, Virginia, in which more than fifty thousand high school students participated.

Patriotism is devotion to your country: to love your country is to love its institutions and values. Patriotism is inherent to good citizenship because all other civic values have their root in the desire to better the country. Patriotism has a special place in the American identity—from the Enlightenment ideals of the Revolution, through Manifest Destiny, through [former president Ronald] Reagan's musings on patriotism in his Farewell Address, Americans have always held patriotism in high esteem for good reason. It is patriotism that unites Americans as a nation and as a people.

One of the greatest documents professing patriotism in American history is *The American Crisis*, a series of essays by Thomas Paine. In his first essay Paine states, "The summer soldier and the sunshine patriot will, in this crisis, shrink from the service of their country; but he that stands it now, deserves the love and thanks of man and woman." He concludes the series by stating "And when we view a flag, which to the eye is beautiful, and to contemplate its rise and origin inspires a sensation of sublime delight, our national honor must unite with our interest to prevent injury to the one, or to insult the other." *The American Crisis* is a call to patriotism; Paine's purpose in writing *The American Crisis* was to encourage American solidarity against Britain in the early and uncer-

Geoffrey Whitener, "Patriotism Fuels and Advances Our Nation," *Human Events*, April 17, 2010. Reproduced by permission.

tain days of America. Were it not for American patriotism, America would not have won the Revolution. The first essay of *The American Crisis* was judged so inspirational that [George] Washington read it aloud to his demoralized troops before the attack on Trenton.

Thomas Paine was a great admirer of George Washington; he described Washington as a "cabinet of fortitude." Washington was quite possibly the greatest American patriot. At a meeting of his officers, after they had urged him to march on Congress, Washington put on a pair of glasses to read a letter. General Washington asked his men to "permit me to put on my spectacles, for I have not only grown gray but almost blind in the service of my country." The officers were touched; any thoughts of a march on Congress died there. Washington's service to America was not for personal gain—it was for the betterment of his nation and his countrymen. Washington had everything to lose in the American Revolution; by being a leading revolutionary, he put his property, life, and honor on the line, with little chance of personal betterment. This is patriotism at its finest. Americans can look to Washington as an example of the greatness of selfless patriotism.

All Citizens Should Demonstrate Patriotism

All citizens should try to demonstrate patriotism in their actions. I hang a flag outside my house to show patriotism. I follow national events, and will vote when I'm of age. And I'm an Eagle Scout. Whenever a scout recites the Scout Oath, he begins with "On my honor, I will do my best to do my duty, to God and my country. . . ." Patriotism is promoted by scouting, because scouting, as a youth development organization, seeks to make better citizens of boys. By being an Eagle Scout, I hope to demonstrate patriotism and encourage others to do the same.

Patriotism is the source of other civic virtues: A patriot is industrious, persistent, respectful, and courageous, because actions that exemplify these and other virtues uplift the country, making it better for everybody. Americans are unlike other nationalities in that we do not share a common ethnicity or religion. Rather, we are united by ideals. We are united by patriotism, devotion to a country that has brought freedom to millions of people. What other country can boast of a revolution based on the ideals of liberty and freedom that did not fall into despotism and chaos? Americans should be patriotic, because patriotism is the force that holds our country together and advances our nation. Patriotism is, ultimately, selflessness for the benefit of other citizens. It is for the benefit of our countrymen and our nation that every American should strive for the highest patriotic ideal.

Patriotism Can Serve Constructive Purposes in Education

Peter Levine

Peter Levine is director of the Center for Information and Research on Civic Learning and Engagement (CIRCLE) and research director of Tufts University's Jonathan M. Tisch College of Citizenship and Public Service. He is the author of several books.

I suspect that most Americans want schools to teach patriotism. However, experts on education are, for the most part, leery of this goal. In a CIRCLE [Center for Information and Research on Civic Learning and Engagement] working paper, William Damon writes:

> The final, and most serious, problem that I will mention has to do with the capacity for positive feelings towards one society, with a sense of attachment, a sense of affiliation, a sense of purpose fostered by one's role as citizen. This is an emotional capacity that, since the time of the ancient Greeks, has been known as patriotism. This is not a familiar word in most educational circles. In fact, I would guess that patriotism is the most politically incorrect word in education today. If you think it's hard to talk about morality and values in schools, try talking about patriotism. You really can't get away with it without provoking an argument or, at the least, a curt change of subject. Teachers too often confuse a patriotic love of country with the kind of militaristic chauvinism that 20th-century dictators used to justify warfare and manipulate their own masses. They do not seem to realize that it was the patriotic resistance to these dictatorships, by citizens of democratic republics such as our own, that saved the world from tyranny in the past century and is the best hope of doing so in the future.

Peter Levine, "Should We Teach Patriotism?" www.PeterLevine.ws, April 11, 2006. www.peterlevine.ws. Reproduced by permission.

Along similar lines, Harry Brighouse quotes a British official, Nick Tate, who complains about his experience on a UK [United Kingdom] curriculum committee: "There was such a widespread association between national identity, patriotism, xenophobia, and racism that it was impossible to talk about the first two without being accused of the rest." The Civic Mission of Schools report (a consensus statement that I helped to organize) does not use the word "patriotism."

The question can be divided into two parts: Is patriotism a desirable attitude? Is it an attitude that should be promoted by public schools? I would answer both questions with a qualified yes.

Being strongly attached to a community or nation as a child increases the odds that you will care enough about it to scrutinize it critically when you become a young adult.

Love of Country Is Like Love of Family

Patriotism is love of country. For most people, it is not a passionate and exclusive and life-altering love. It's more like love for a blood relative, perhaps an aunt. It doesn't involve choice. It doesn't require a tremendously high estimate of the object's intrinsic qualities. (You may admire Mother Teresa more than your Aunt Teresa, but it is the latter you love.) It implies a sense of obligation, including an obligation to understand and be interested in the object. It also implies a sense of entitlement: You can expect your own aunt, or your nation, to help you in ways that others need not. Both the obligation and the entitlement arise because of a sense of identification, a "we-ness," a seeing of yourself in the object and vice versa.

I think that people should love large human communities in this way. You may put your family first, but to love *only* them is too exclusive. Loving all of humankind is good, but it doesn't mean the same thing as love for a concrete object. For instance, you cannot have an obligation to know many details about humankind.

A nation works as an object of love. One can identify with it and feel consequent obligations and entitlements, including the obligation to know its history, culture, constitution, and geography. Love for a country inspires, enlarges one's sympathies, and gives one a sense of support and solidarity. I would not claim that these moral advantages follow *only* from loving a country. One can also love world Jewry, one's city, or one's fellow Rotarians. But love of country has some particular advantages:

1. Patriotism promotes participation in national politics, including such acts as voting, joining national social movements, litigating in federal court, and enlisting in the military or serving in the civil service. In turn, broad participation makes national politics work better and more justly. And national politics is important, because national institutions have supremacy. A system that devolved more power to localities would need less national participation, and hence less patriotism. But it would have its own disadvantages.

2. Patriotism is a flexible concept, subject to fruitful debate. Consider what love of America meant for [singer-songwriter] Woody Guthrie, Francis Bellamy (the Christian socialist author of the Pledge of Allegiance), Frederick Douglass (author of a great 1852 Independence Day speech), Nathan Hale, Presidents Lincoln and Reagan, [FBI director] J. Edgar Hoover, [novelist] Saul Bellow, or [philosopher] Richard Rorty. All these men believed that they could make effective political arguments by citing—and redefining—patriotic sentiments. One could argue that their rhetoric obfuscated: They should have defended their core values without mixing in patriotic sentiments. Brighouse complains that patrio-

tism can be "used to interrupt the flow of free and rational political debate within a country." But I am not so much of a rationalist as to believe that there exist stand-alone arguments for all moral principles. Rather, reasonable political debate involves allusions and reinterpretations of shared traditions; and patriotism provides a rich and diverse store.

3. It seems to me that a democratic government can legitimately decide to instill love of country, whereas it cannot legitimately make people love world Jewry or the Rotary Club. Local democratic governments can also promote love of their own local communities, and that is common enough—but it doesn't negate the right of a national democracy to promote patriotism.

4. Patriotism has a role in a theory of human development that Damon has elsewhere defended. This theory holds that being strongly attached to a community or nation as a child increases the odds that you will care enough about it to scrutinize it critically when you become a young adult. In my own case, as a young boy in the [President Richard] Nixon era, I thought G-Men [FBI agents] were heroes and wanted to be one. Now I am a strong civil libertarian. I believe my initial attachment to the US has kept me from simply withdrawing from it. . . . However, I'm just one person—and a white, male, middle-class person who has been treated justly by the state. Damon's developmental theory may not work as well for children who face evident injustice.

Thus, as a moral sentiment, patriotism has benefits. However, it can also encourage exclusivity or an illegitimate preference for one's fellow citizens over other human beings. Like all forms of love, it can blind you to faults. These problems are serious, but they can be addressed. After all, some forms of American patriotism identify our particular nation with inclusiveness and the fair treatment of foreign countries.

Teaching Patriotism in Schools Raises Problems

The teaching of patriotism in public schools raises special problems, several of which Harry Brighouse explores in Chapter V of *On Education*. Here I mention the two most serious concerns:

1. Legitimate government rests on the sincere or authentic consent of the governed. If the state uses its great power over public school students to promote love of itself, that consent is inauthentic. Brighouse: "The education system is an agent of the state; if we allow the state to use that system to produce sentiments in the populace which are designed to win consent for it, it thereby taints whatever consent it subsequently enjoys as being non-legitimizing."

This is a serious concern, requiring constant vigilance; but I believe it should be put in context. Schools do not have a monopoly on students' attention. They compete against politicians (many of whom love to denounce the national government), religious leaders (who believe that true sovereignty is God's), and big commercial advertisers (who promote consumption instead of political engagement). Within schools there are plenty of teachers and administrators who hold negative views of the national government. I think the dangers of brainwashing are slight, and it's helpful to present students with an ideal—patriotism in its various forms—that they and their teachers can argue with.

2. A patriotic presentation of history requires whitewashing and distorting the truth about what happened and why. For instance [Brighouse says] "an educator who has anywhere in her mind the purposes of instilling love of country will have a hard time teaching about the causal process which led up to the Civil War in the US." That's because pursuit of the truth requires one to consider that the Civil War was perhaps fought for economic reasons—a dispiriting thought for a patriot. Likewise, Brighouse thinks that textbooks depict [civil

111

rights activist] Rosa Parks as a "tired seamstress" instead of a "political agitator" because the former view (while false) better supports patriotism.

Obviously, Brighouse has a point—but a close look at his cases shows how complicated the issue is. For example, as an American patriot, I find it deeply moving that Rosa Parks was trained at the Highlander Folk School, whose founder, Myles Horton, was inspired by [Nobel Peace Prize winner] Jane Addams, whose father, John (double-D) Addams was a young colleague and follower of Abe Lincoln in the Illinois State legislature. That's only one lineage and heritage in the story of Rosa Parks. It is, however, a deeply American and patriotically "Whiggish" one—and it's truer than the cliché of a tired seamstress. It connects Parks to the profound patriotism of Lincoln (who redefined the American past at Gettysburg) and the pacifist patriotism of Jane Addams.

Ham-fisted efforts to make kids patriotic can backfire. But rigorous investigations of history can make kids patriotic.

In any case, why study Parks at all unless one has a special attachment to the United States? If the issue is simply nonviolence, then one should study Aung San Suu Kyi [Burmese politician and Nobel Peace Prize recipient], who is still very much alive and in need of support. I think every young American should know the true story of Rosa Parks, and my reasons are essentially patriotic.

To put the matter more generally: History should be taught truthfully, but it must also be taught selectively. There is no such thing as a neutral or truly random selection of topics. Selecting topics in order to promote patriotism seems fine to me, as long as the love-of-country that we promote is a realistic one with ethical limitations.

Finally, the causal mechanisms here are a little unpredictable. Ham-fisted efforts to make kids patriotic can backfire. But rigorous investigations of history can make kids patriotic. I always think of my own experience helping local students (all children of color) conduct oral-history interviews about segregation in their own school system. They learned that people like them had been deliberately excluded for generations. They took away the lesson that their schools were worth fighting over, that kids could play an active role in history, and that their community was interesting. One girl told a friend from the more affluent neighboring county, "You have the Mall, but we have the history!"

Again, the purpose of our lesson was not simply to teach historical truth and method, but also to increase students' attachment to a community. We were like educators who try to inculcate patriotism, except that we were interested in a county rather than the nation. Our pedagogy involved helping kids to uncover a history of *injustice*. The result was an increase in local attachment. The moral is that truth and patriotism may have a complex and contingent relationship, but they are not enemies.

Patriotism Is Misunderstood by Its Opponents

Bookworm

The blogger Bookworm is the proprietor of the Bookworm Room website and also writes elsewhere on the web.

"I only regret that I have but one life to lose for my country"

> —*Nathan Hale, upon his execution in 1776.*

"It is rather for us to be here dedicated to the great task remaining before us—that from these honored dead we take increased devotion to that cause for which they gave the last full measure of devotion—that we here highly resolve that these dead shall not have died in vain—that this nation, under God, shall have a new birth of freedom—and that government of the people, by the people, for the people, shall not perish from the earth."

> —*Abraham Lincoln, giving the Gettysburg Address in 1863.*

"Ask not what your country can do for you; ask what you can do for your country."

> —*John F. Kennedy, giving his 1961 inaugural address.*

"The entire country may disagree with me, but I don't understand the necessity for patriotism. Why do you have to be a patriot? About what? This land is our land? Why? You can like where you live and like your life, but as for loving the whole country . . . I don't see why people care about patriotism."

> —*Natalie Maines, Dixie Chick extraordinaire,*
> *spilling her guts to the British press in June 2006.*

Do you remember that old Sesame Street song? The one that goes, "One of these things is not like the other one. One of these things just doesn't belong." It's pretty easy here

Bookworm, "Patriotism and Anti-Patriotism," *American Thinker*, July 4, 2006. Reproduced by permission.

to pick Ms. Maines out from two centuries of Americans who believed that our country was and is something special. Now that it's July 4th, her self-centered comments got me thinking about patriotism in the modern era.

Part of why patriotism has gone out the window for so many Americans—especially young ones—is because we live in an age where self-sacrifice, rather than being considered noble, is merely considered stupid.

As always, it's useful to start by focusing on the word itself. The dictionary defines "patriotism" as "love of and devotion to one's country" (the *American Heritage Dictionary*) or "love of country and willingness to sacrifice for it" (WordNet). Although the first three quotations I've included are more emotive than the dictionaries' dry language, they mean precisely the same thing: Patriotism is an individuals' belief that his country is so special that saving it is worth sacrifice.

Natalie Maines, however, is the voice of the new American. First of all, she's staggeringly self-centered. It's all about Natalie: Do what you want, live where you want. As for anyone else's wants and needs, well, the hell with 'em. This is all about me, me, me.

So, we can conclude that part of why patriotism has gone out the window for so many Americans—especially young ones—is because we live in an age where self-sacrifice, rather than being considered noble, is merely considered stupid. Why do something for your country, as [President John F.] Kennedy requested, when you can use the same time to get a latte and a massage?

There's also a huge dollop of multicultural guilt thrown into the fact that Ms. Maines questions whether "this land is our land?" Natalie's been raised to believe that we stole this land from the Native Americans and have no right to it. Even without the stain of America's treatment of the indigenous population thrown into the mix, you just know that Natalie believes that we white, imperialist, ugly Americans really don't qualify to call any land our own. Our legacy should be one of shame, not patriotism.

However, I don't see Ms. Maines volunteering to give anything back. She likes the perks of life that our capitalist system has created, and I don't see her riding the plains and killing her own food. It's enough merely to hate what she is and where she comes from.

A state-coerced patriotism . . . utterly negates the love and self-sacrifice for the greater good that characterizes the patriotism that drove Patrick Henry, Abraham Lincoln, and Edith Cavell.

Ms. Maines isn't the most articulate girl on the block, nor the deepest thinker, so I'll add two more things that I think color modern anti-patriotism. First, I think the *Deutschland über alles* [Germany above all] patriotism that characterized the Nazis has left a lasting legacy, especially liberals. Thus, liberals believe that love of one's country is the inevitable first step to concentration camps and dreams of world domination. Indeed, if you rewrite my last sentence so that "Gitmo" [referreing to Guantánamo Bay detention facility in Cuba] replaces "concentration camps" and "Iraq" replaces "world," you've basically spelled out the Left's fear of patriotism. To them, it's impossible for patriotism to be a celebration of what's good about America; instead, it is inevitably the beginning of totalitarianism.

If you think about this analysis, though, you realize that it puts the cart before the horse. It's not that patriotism leads to totalitarianism. It's that totalitarianism relies on blind patriotism to control people, and keep their focus away from the complete absence of freedom. Indeed, British nurse Edith Cavell, whom the Germans executed during WWI [World War

I], spoke before her death about a pure form of patriotism: "Standing as I do in view of God and Eternity, I realise that patriotism is not enough, I must have no hatred or bitterness towards anyone."

True Patriotism Is the Opposite of Totalitarianism

In other words, true patriotism, not mere jingoism, or racism, is the opposite of state-imposed thought, aimed at deflecting attention from the state and focusing it on the "other." A state-coerced patriotism—"salute the flag or be whipped"; "hang a flag in front of your house or go to a gulag [forced labor camps]"; "'volunteer' for a 25-year stint in the military or be executed"; "blow up women and children to make a point"—utterly negates the love and self-sacrifice for the greater good that characterizes the patriotism that drove [lawyer and politician] Patrick Henry, Abraham Lincoln, and Edith Cavell. Instead, they'd simply be meaningless motions at gunpoint.

Second, uncomplicated American patriotism may simply have died on the spittle flecked streets of American cities in the late 1960s and early 1970s. That was when hippies screaming "My Lai" battled it out with construction workers hollering "My country right or wrong" or "America, love it or leave it." The problem with the latter slogans is that, while they tried pithily to express myriad complex beliefs about what America is and what patriotism means, they ended up being pretty unappealing concepts. The first implies that America has no obligation to look to a moral compass to guide her (bye-bye [composer] Irving Berlin's "God Bless America" with its idea about God guiding America to do the right thing). The second slogan apparently demands the same mindless obedience that one would see in a totalitarian regime. Once patriotism became entangled in those sayings, it was cheapened.

What we're left with is the question: Is patriotism okay? I think it is. If we don't believe that there are core values and qualities that make America someplace special—as distinguished from Ms. Maines's belief that you can go anywhere and get what you have here—then the concept of nationhood becomes entirely meaningless. And while liberals may envision some halcyon world government, guided by a beneficent Kofi Annan [former secretary-general of the United Nations], what will actually happen without any coalescing force is social and cultural chaos. People need something in which to believe, and the vacuum left behind by abandoning our own belief in ourselves will quickly be filled in a way that will leave Ms. Maines and her ilk yearning for the America she's so blithely castigating today.

So, hang up your flag, attend your parade, and say "God Bless America," not because the state or I are telling you to, but because you believe, as I do, that while America may not be perfect, she's still the best game around.

Nations Should Not Be Valued Merely for Their Own Sake

Ilya Somin

Ilya Somin is an associate professor of law at George Mason University in Arlington, Virginia. His articles have appeared in many national publications.

It is now widely recognized that extreme nationalism often causes great harm, increasing the risk of war and human rights violations. But even if nationalism is often an evil, perhaps patriotism can still be good. Patriotism is certainly distinguishable from nationalism defined as loyalty to one's own nation-state based on ties of language, culture, or ethnicity. It also differs from nationalism defined as a sense of moral obligation to members of one's ethnic or racial group across national boundaries. In common usage, patriotism generally means loyalty to one's government and/or its ideals regardless of ethnic or racial identity. For example, one can be a patriotic American even if you are a member of an ethnic minority, English is not your native language, and you dislike mainstream American popular culture.

To the extent that patriotism simply means supporting your country when its government promotes good ideals and policies, I'm all in favor of it. Indeed, I admire the American political system because, despite serious flaws, it provides a great deal of freedom and happiness to large numbers of people. I also admire it because, unlike most other nations, it is not primarily based on ties of race, language, or ethnicity.

At the same time, I am opposed to patriotism in the sense of valuing a nation or government for its own sake. Unlike some, I don't believe that we should "love" our country in the

Ilya Somin, "On Patriotism," *Volokh Conspiracy*, December 2, 2009. Volokh.com. Reproduced by permission.

same unconditional way that we love a spouse or family member. That kind of commitment too readily leads people to support governments that are oppressive and unjust. More fundamentally, it loses sight of the principle that governments and nations are means, not ends in themselves. The Founding Fathers got it right when they wrote in the Preamble to the Constitution that they were creating a new government in order to "establish justice, insure domestic tranquility, provide for the common defense, promote the general welfare, and secure the blessings of liberty to ourselves and our posterity." The Constitution and the United States generally are not ends in themselves, but means to the objectives laid out in the Preamble. The corollary is that the government deserves patriotic loyalty only insofar as it promotes those objectives better than the available alternatives. If I thought that freedom, happiness and other important values could be better achieved by replacing the United States with some other political entity or by breaking it up through secession, I would not support maintaining the status quo out of patriotism. To do so would be to exalt a mere means above the ends it is supposed to serve.

Affection for Government Is Only a Means to an End

Some, like prominent blogger and legal scholar Glenn Reynolds, argue that we need "irrational affection" for government in order for it to work well. I am skeptical. A population that values its government for purely instrumental reasons can still give it the necessary support and defend it against external enemies. At the same time, it is less likely to tolerate abuses of government power on the grounds that we have a patriotic duty to support the state for its own sake. But even if some degree of "irrational affection" for government is necessary, it should still be regarded as a means to an end, not a value in itself.

Ultimately, I think the right attitude towards patriotism was best captured by Milton Friedman in his 1962 book *Capitalism and Freedom*:

> In a much quoted passage in his inaugural address, President [John F.] Kennedy said, "Ask not what your country can do for you—ask what you can do for your country. . . ." Neither half of the statement expresses a relation between the citizen and his government that is worthy of the ideals of free men in a free society. The paternalistic "what your country can do for you" implies that the government is the patron, the citizen the ward, a view that is at odds with the free man's belief in his own responsibility for his own destiny. The organismic, "what you can do for your country" implies that the government is the master or the deity, the citizen, the servant or the votary. To the free man, the country is the collection of individuals who compose it, not something over and above them. . . . [H]e regards government as a means, an instrumentality, neither a grantor of favors and gifts, nor a master or god to be blindly worshipped and served.
>
> The free man will ask neither what his country can do for him nor what he can do for his country. He will ask rather "What can I and my compatriots do through government" to . . . advance our several goals and purposes, and above all, to protect our freedom? And he will accompany this question with another: How can we keep the government we create from becoming a Frankenstein that will destroy the very freedom we establish it to protect?

Patriotism Conflicts with the Idea That Government Exists to Serve the People

George Kateb

George Kateb is a professor emeritus at Princeton University, where he was formerly director of the Program in Political Philosophy. He is the author of many books, most recently Patriotism and Other Mistakes.

Patriotism is love of country. What kind of love is that? Some defenders of patriotism who want us to love our country use such terms as fatherland and mother country. Such usage seems to indicate that we should love our country as we love our parents. Do they mean that a country is a person and should be loved as a person is loved? Obviously a country is not a person. There is a metaphor involved. If we notice the metaphor, we see that what we are doing when we liken a country to a parent is performing an act of the imagination. More commonly, the metaphor is not understood as a metaphor. Rather, many people just accept the usage as if it were natural and can and should go without examination. They manage to do two contradictory things simultaneously: They know that of course a country is not a person, yet they act with energy on the belief that it is. The metaphor facilitates an exploitable mental confusion.

Let us repel the metaphors of fatherland and mother country by thinking about love of parents. We might find that it would be fairly monstrous to love a country as one already loves one's parents (or conversely to model love of parents on the love we are urged to feel for our country). I love my parents—if I do—because I began my life in infant attachment to

George Kateb, "On Patriotism," *Cato Unbound*, March 10, 2008. Reproduced by permission.

them, well before I had a sense of self and a developed mind. They "imprinted" themselves on me; we bonded; only pain ensued from their neglect or abuse, while I was content if they wrapped me in their enfolding nurturant love. As I grew, I realized that I would be lost without them; I was wholly dependent on them; I loved them. With the onset of maturity, I felt gratitude towards them. I knew that without them there would literally have been no me. Love of parents is an obligation that is more than an obligation and should not be felt as one, except under the most trying circumstances. Love should overwhelm all feelings of reluctant duty. Despite conflicts and frustrations I loved my parents; if the difficulties were too great and I became alienated or even hostile, my feelings would remain at least ambivalent. (Is there ambivalence from the start?) I realized that alienation or hostility was an open wound; only reconciliation could heal it. Perhaps it could never be healed, to my inestimable loss.

Are such feelings properly transferred to a country? Should love of country overwhelm all self-centered reluctance? In particular, is gratitude, a kind of love, the right emotion to feel towards one's country? Although children are not usually asked to die for their parents, and most parents wouldn't accept the offer if it were made, some defenders of patriotism imagine the state as a super-parent that may ask its children to die for it. The idea of patriotism is inseparable from killing and dying for your country. A good patriot is a good killer.

All defenses of patriotism finally rest on the rejection of the idea of individual self-ownership.

I do not literally owe to my country my coming into existence. It's true that I could not go on if I didn't live in some society, but my genes are not politically identifiable; a country is not a biological entity. My parents could have moved after I was born; my country could have lost the territory in which I was born; I could have been abducted and raised elsewhere. My parents are one thing, my country another, altogether different. A country would not exist without its people; the reverse is literally false and appears true only by metaphorical distortion. . . .

Some Claim People Are Owned by Their Country

The best recent defense of patriotism, Maurizio Viroli's "For Love of Country: An Essay on Patriotism and Nationalism," bases itself on the metaphor of country as fatherland, as fidelity to the legacy of the political fathers, who are supposed to bind succeeding generations by a kind of filial piety. An intensely American philosopher, William James (in "The Moral Equivalent of War"), can think that it is good for young people especially to feel that they are "owned" by their country. I find it surprising that such a clear-headed thinker, democratic through and through, can voice such a view. But the much larger surprise is that we find in him, where we shouldn't, a defense of the idea that, being owned, we owe the state or the country a debt, a "blood-tax" that must be paid when the state demands it. A blood-tax, however, isn't an exaction of gratitude. Rather, the patriotic heroism of dying prematurely or risking death is the best definition of being a man. If James doesn't follow [Ancient Greek philosopher] Socrates in saying that the state, as our parent, gives us our lives, he exceeds Socrates by suggesting that in being owned by the state, we owe it a blood-tax, not merely a grateful readiness to die when it commands. For James, only death or its risk proves patriotism.

Socrates' position in the *Crito* and the sentiment expressed by William James and other advocates of patriotism share the idea that we do not own ourselves. We come into the world already obliged after a certain age to serve the country and feel patriotic passions for it. I associate this notion with traditions of thinking that have not yet arrived at the idea that political society owes its rightful existence only to the consent of the people, originally and continuously thereafter. Through consent, the people own the state, which is its servant, not its parent or owner. The premise is the principle that each person owns himself or herself. From self-ownership is derived the idea of political consent, freely given or withheld or withdrawn, and it is formulated variously by theorists of the social contract, from the seventeenth century and after.... The most formidable social contract is the United States Constitution. I hazard the thought that all defenses of patriotism finally rest on the rejection of the idea of individual self-ownership, even though people have patriotic feelings that can and do emerge without the assistance of any theoretical defense.

The theoretical debate about patriotism directly interests only thinkers who concern themselves with questions of political and moral philosophy, and publicists who are eager to promote some policy or other.

The common thread in contract theory is that the obligation to obey can derive only from consent, expressed or tacit, and always given by the individual, whether as a personal pledge or a pledge given in association with other like-minded people. Every person is born equally free by the very nature of his or her humanity. The first enemy of the social contract is therefore patriarchy, the assertion that the state, usually a hereditary monarchy, exists by the will and grace of God; the ruler is father of his country; as father, the king rules without consent, just as children did not and could not choose their father (or mother); as patriarch, what is more, the king owns the people of the kingdom and their property. They belong to him and they ought to feel grateful for his protection. The king's only obligation is to God; otherwise he may dispose of the people and their goods as he sees fit. In battle with this outlook, the theorists of the social contract tried to kill not the king exactly, but the view that the king is father in the image of the God who is the lord and father of mankind, the source of life and death.

Others Say Consent to Live in a Country Creates an Obligation to Die for It

A great irony is that, try as it might, the theory of the social contract never wrestled free of the claim that the people owe their existence to the state and hence that the state owns the people. While the contract theorists unmistakably struggle to establish the proposition the state does not own the people, they nevertheless also say—and I think, inconsistently—that it can require citizens to die to preserve it. All the theorists accept this requirement. It is as if by eroding the idea that the king is father and owner of the people and owes his authority to God's grace, they feel the compensatory need to replace devotion to the king by some other bond that would yield a *moral* obligation to sacrifice oneself for the state. The claim is that such a bond is created by a person's consent to live under a state. The basis of the state in rational choice is turned into the basis for morally allowing the state to cause the death or the risk of death of citizens. Our choice to preserve our lives is turned by the contract theorists into a choice to assume an obligation to die for the sake of what supposedly, in the first place, exists in order to preserve us. Necessity gives birth to the state but the state gives birth to another kind of necessity, which is a dangerous and recurrently lethal necessity. The state for all does not preserve all lives, and loses or wastes a good many.

There is cruelty lodged in the heart of the theory of the social contract, even though it seeks to demystify the state and to replace the traditional awe of the parent-state by clear-sighted understanding of the state's rational purpose. The language of obligation supersedes the language of gratitude and devotion. But the mentality of self-sacrifice perhaps takes on a greater strength when it is made to flow logically from the obligation that choice creates. The social contract tends to become a more ingenious trap than any appeal to the patriotic love of country rooted in filial loyalty, whether in its pure Socratic form or in the various dilutions of it that are always current. Just because parents usually don't ask their children to die for them, and consider it an unspeakable tragedy when any child dies before [his or her] parents, the metaphor of the state as parent must contradict its literal source: Parents feel horror at the death of their children. The theory of the social contract must confront and try to overcome a different contradiction: A contract for life is also, and inevitably, a contract for (premature violent) death. The upshot is that the social contract can become a more bloodthirsty theory, despite its apparent dispassion, than the idea of the parent-state (or owner-state), because its contradiction seems more successfully resolvable on the theoretical level. Children are not supposed to die for their parents but equals are supposed to die for one another.

Yet the theorists of contract knew that consent would not supply the passionate energy that is required to discharge the obligation to die. . . .

Patriotism is the greatest asset in the internal and ever-present war against the sentiments and institutions of free government.

[Eighteenth-century French philosopher Jean-Jacques] Rousseau in *The Social Contract* asserts that by dying to preserve the city, its citizens are merely giving back to the state what they received from it. In his theoretical desperation, he thus returns us to the pre-contract idea that the state owns the people: because it has given them life, it may take life away from them, if need be. To this old mystique, Rousseau then adds the enlightened rational calculation that without a state, they would have had to risk their lives in the anarchic condition in an eventually vain attempt to preserve them. Don't people gain from collective strength? Don't they reduce their chances of dying by living in a political system that their consent has created? Yes, they do—that is, some do, but some don't. The dead have been sacrificed for others, and therefore the whole egalitarian logic of the social contract is violated by a majoritarian calculation. It is a best bargain only for those who live, not for those who died before their time. And so Rousseau works to bypass the dilemma by advocating a tight communal life infused with patriotic love of country. His theory is a tremendous effort to make political life more fair and less arbitrary. But in many respects the life he advocates is finally not more rational. It is as irrationally based in devotion and gratitude to the city as other societies are, or even more so. Even worse, his theory may seduce us, by its promise of justice, to grant the blood-tax it levies. I doubt, however, that Rousseau's version of the blood-tax joined to his sketch of the best bargain can succeed in theoretically reconciling the social contract with the obligation to die for the state.

Patriotism Weakens the Belief That Government Is a Servant to the People

If neither the metaphor of the parent-state nor the idea of the people's consent to government can justify killing and dying for the state, patriotism has not run out of resources. Whatever theory says, patriotism will prevail. One main reason is that it is a usually tacit ideology and flourishes without philosophical assistance. The theoretical debate about patriotism directly interests only thinkers who concern themselves with questions of political and moral philosophy, and publicists who are eager to promote some policy or other. The debate about patriotism reaches undeniably to some of the most profound speculative matters, yet patriotism itself proceeds as a brute fact of life. The trouble is that this brute fact contributes to the erosion of the sentiment that government exists by consent and has the status of servant to the people. Modern liberty can't do without the premise that government rightfully exists only by means of popular consent to a system of government that routinely works through continuous popular consent. The point is to show that patriotism facilitates the erosion of the idea of rational consent, and does so by means of an improvident and unreasoned acceptance of a second social contract that usurps and inhabits the body of the original one that created the system of constitutional democracy.

If no one were a patriot, the world would be better off than it now is.

The brute fact of patriotism is made brute by the inveterate inclination in men to associate virility with the exertion involved in killing and risking death. No theory can ever defeat or discredit this inclination, which helps to engender the fantasy that the competition of political units is the highest kind of team sports. Men love teams, love to live in a world where they are called on to back or play for their team against other teams, even though the sport of war is soaked in blood. Socratic notions of gratitude or Jamesian notions of infinite indebtedness are not necessary for this love. In the sport, where aristocrats used to play their games, elites now mobilize groups or masses to slaughter each other. Men can become peace-loving for a while, but not forever. The women who love them encourage their inclination to see team sports as the essence of their masculinity, and to call patriotic this inclination when it is projected into politics. The pity is that men lend their energies to a state that sooner or later embarks on an inherently unjust imperialist career and thus gets constantly engaged in policies that are deliberated in secrecy, and sustained by secrecy and propaganda, and removed from meaningful public deliberation. Patriotism is indispensable for sustaining this career of anti-democracy.

In general, an activist foreign policy works tirelessly to de-legitimate any constitutional democracy. Patriotism is the greatest asset in the internal and ever-present war against the sentiments and institutions of free government. The support of one's team is not the defense of the Constitution. What gets hollowed out is government by rational consent, while a number of basic freedoms are steadily attenuated. The original contract for constitutional democracy is usurped, and re-placed, in significant part, by a second contract for expansion and predation. It is bad enough that the original contract is interpreted to mandate dying for one's country. Much worse is the displacement of the original contract. The spoils of activism and imperialism intensify political and economic inequality while immunizing leaders from their accountability to citizens to an ever-greater extent. Citizens become followers. Leaders and followers live in different worlds. Citizens allow the patriotic thrill of team sports to obscure the radical alteration that descends on the original contract, while acquiescing in the gains of large and sometimes sinister interests that use patriotism in their appeals for support. The great theorists of the social contract would have been horrified; they didn't quite have such a drastic mutation in mind—not to mention the anti-imperialist Socrates in his espousal of the parent-state.

Patriotism, more than any other passion in political life, makes virtues do the work of vices while promoting the praise of vices as disguised virtues. It thus sustains enormous moral perversity. If no one were a patriot, the world would be better off than it now is, when almost all are patriots. Theorists shouldn't join in.

The Cultivation of Patriotism by Governments Never Leads to Good

The Radix

The Radix *is a blog containing a series of debates on legal, political, cultural, and sociological issues.*

George Bernard Shaw [a Nobel Prize–winning Irish playwright] once famously remarked that patriotism was the conviction that one's country was superior to all others, simply because one was born in it. Strictly speaking, of course, patriotism is the love of one's country, and a person may love his country without necessarily thinking it superior. But truth be told, it generally does involve precisely such feelings.

Man is a social animal, and has coalesced in groups of one form or another throughout the ages, with loyalties to tribes and clans, city-states, religions and ethnic groups. The modern nation-state is a fairly new innovation, and its viability depends to some extent on a shared identity and loyalty to the polity. The problem arises when patriotism is raised to high principle, when it becomes an orthodoxy.

The False Religion of Patriotism

There are several problems with patriotism. The first relates to the typical notion of superiority. The sense of identity essential to a deeply felt and passionate patriotism relies upon differentiation with the cultures and the social realities of other states. It depends on the judgment that we are better than them. This typically involves nationalistic mythologizing, which is a form of self-deception, and at the end of the day

The Radix, "The False Religion of Patriotism," The Radix.net, November 22, 2009. Reproduced by permission.

the entire belief system is irrational—just as all gods cannot be the one true god, so all states cannot be superior to all the others.

This nationalistic sense of superiority, and corresponding denigration and discounting of the rights of the peoples of other nations, creates the conditions in which conflict is so much more likely. It is so easily manipulated by those in power to drag the nation into war. [Nazi military leader Hermann] Goering understood this well.

Second, as patriotism becomes an increasing orthodoxy, it entirely stifles the political discourse and debate so necessary to democracy. "My country, right or wrong" forecloses discussion. Any criticism of policy is attacked and suffocated as being unpatriotic. Consider the atmosphere in the U.S.A. shortly after 9/11 [September 11, 2001, terrorist attacks on the United States] when the few people who tried to ask questions about the "root causes" for the attack were utterly vilified. [Television host] Bill Maher was almost fired for an 'unpatriotic' comment. Even in the run-up to the invasion of Iraq, the few who questioned the wisdom or legality of the war, were marginalized.

Third, once mobilized, patriotism begins to become self-perpetuating in a society. Like a religion, it becomes entrenched, working its way ever more deeply into the fabric of the culture, and develops into dogma. It can become ludicrous. Consider the issue of Barak Obama being chastised over not wearing an American flag lapel pin during the campaign—to the point that he ended up feeling compelled to wear one.

So when governments begin taking steps to consciously cultivate and foster increased patriotism, we should be concerned. Japan, for instance, revised its Basic Act on Education a few years ago, to make the inculcation of patriotism a primary and concrete objective of the education system. And so, the descendents of the Sun Goddess, just like the Master Race of Aryans, the people of Manifest Destiny and American Exceptionalism, and the Han peoples of the Middle Kingdom, to name but a few, can learn that they are really superior to everyone else. That never leads anywhere good.

Humanity and the Nation-State

Patriotism relies upon a sense of superiority that can create hostility and conflict; it stifles internal debate; it is a self-perpetuating meme within a culture; and therefore we should be concerned when governments try to mobilize and exploit it. Beta [my debate partner] addresses none of these.

But he does make an assertion that is insupportable—that love of country is one of those "modes of socialization" that is necessary to our very humanity. This cannot be right. Now, I conceded in my own argument that man is a social animal, for which the loyalties to various groups and collective entities have been crucial throughout history. That is certainly part of our evolutionary makeup, as [my opponent] Beta asserts. But there is no basis for arguing that the nation-state, the "country" of our times, is an entity to which we must develop such "love" in order to fully express our humanity.

The territorial state is a modern innovation, emerging in the 17th century, and the nation-state newer still. It was not until the 19th century that a true sense of nationalism developed, and was deliberately mobilized by statesmen. And by nationalism here I mean the understanding that the political entity of the territorial state, and the culturally distinct people or nation that inhabit it, are and ought to be congruent. We have only lived in such nation-states for some 150 years, and the fact is that we have lived without the modern sense of patriotism for most of our history.

Of course, as any casual reader of [William] Shakespeare will attest, there has been love and loyalty for other political and social entities. My point is that we could be just as human, derive our collective sense of past, present and future, by mobilizing a sense of affection, loyalty and common bond, for some more cosmopolitan conception than the nation-state. The nation-state relies to some degree on a certain level of patriotism, but our humanity most surely does not depend upon love of the nation-state.

CHAPTER 4

Should Flag Burning Be Banned by Law?

Overview: Most Americans Want Flag Burning Banned but Say It Has Low Priority

Paul Taylor

Paul Taylor is the executive vice president of the Pew Research Center and serves as the director of the center's Social & Demographic Trends project.

About two in three Americans fly the flag. Nearly three in four say flag burning should be illegal. Roughly half say it should be unconstitutional.

But despite these protective instincts, there's been no public clamor demanding that Congress take steps to defend Old Glory against burners and desecrators.

In a nationwide Fox News survey taken earlier this month [June 2006], flag burning ranked a distant last among five issues tested as priorities for Congress this summer. Iraq was first at 35%, followed by gas prices (28%), immigration (26%) and same-sex marriage (5%). Not even one percent of voters said that a flag-burning amendment should be Congress's top priority.

An NBC News/*Wall Street Journal* poll this month asked a different variant of this question. It included flag burning among seven issues and asked registered voters which *two* would be most important in helping them decide how to vote for Congress this fall. Flag burning again came in dead last— with just 4% naming it as their first or second most important issue.

The Pew Research Center took a third approach. In a nationwide telephone [survey] conducted from June 14–19, registered voters were asked whether or not they considered each of 19 issues to be important to them personally. Education led the way (82% said it is "very important"), followed by the economy (80%) and health care (79%). Just under half (49%) said a flag amendment is very important, placing it 14th on the list.

To be sure, even at that level of support, the public judges flag burning to be more important than several other high-profile issues, including global warming, abortion and gay marriage.

Of all the issues tested in the Pew survey, a proposed flag-burning amendment is the one that generated the biggest opinion gap between lower- and higher-educated respondents. Some two-thirds (67%) of those with a high school education or less say flag burning is a very important issue, compared with just 28% of college graduates who say this. There is also a notable partisan division; 60% of Republicans say it is a very important issue, compared with just 44% of Democrats and independents.

Constitutional Amendment

Even though few Americans appear to believe that Old Glory is in the sort of peril that requires high-priority congressional attention, most do support protective measures. Some 73% of the public thinks flag burning should be illegal, according to a Fox News poll this month.

On the question of whether that protection should extend to enactment of a constitutional amendment, the public is divided. A CNN poll earlier this month found 56% in favor of a constitutional amendment. A new Gallup poll similarly found respondents, by a 56%–41% margin, favoring "a constitutional amendment that would allow Congress and state governments to make it illegal to burn the American flag." However, that level of support is considerably lower than the 71% and 68% recorded by Gallup in 1989 and 1990, respectively.

Moreover, when the question in the latest Gallup poll was rephrased for half the sample to ask if the respondent felt that the US Constitution should be amended to make it illegal to burn or desecrate the American flag "as a form of political dissent," the majority shifted, with 45% saying yes to an amendment and 54% saying no.

Still, a 45% level of support for any constitutional amendment is not to be lightly dismissed, given the fact that many people set a high bar for amending the Constitution. For example, while 54% of the public oppose the legalization of gay marriage, just 32% support a constitutional amendment to do so, according to a Pew poll.

Ever since 1989, when the US Supreme Court ruled 5–4 that desecrating the flag is a constitutionally protected form of free speech, Congress has periodically taken up a flag-burning amendment. Last night [June 27, 2006] it came as close as ever to approving one; the Senate's 66–34 vote in favor was just one vote shy of the two-thirds majority required to send such an amendment to the states for ratification.

Flying the Flag

No matter what happened in Congress, many Americans will be flying Old Glory, not just on the coming July 4th holiday, but at various times throughout the year. Some 64% of adults say they display the flag at their home, in their office or on their car, according to a 2005 Pew survey. This figure is down somewhat from 2002, when, in the wake of the September 11 attacks, the number of Americans who said they displayed the flag spiked to 75%. However, the 2005 figure is somewhat higher than levels registered by similar surveys taken in the 1980s and 1990s.

The 2005 survey also found that Old Glory gets its heaviest workout in rural areas. Some three-quarters of rural residents (76%) say they display a flag, compared with 65% of suburbanites and 54% of city dwellers. Also, more Republicans (78%) report displaying the flag than do Democrats (57%) or independents (60%).

The vast majority of Americans consider themselves to be patriotic. In a 2003 Pew survey, more than nine in ten either completely (56%) or mostly (35%) agreed with the statement: "I am very patriotic."

These days, however, very few people conflate patriotism with support for the Iraq war. A CBS News poll taken this past March found that 83% of respondents said they believed someone can be patriotic even if they don't support the war, while just 12% disagreed. Back in May 2004, in response to a slightly different question in a Pew survey, 22% said it was unpatriotic to criticize the war; while 23% said it was patriotic and 49% said neither.

Patriotic Yes, but Culturally Superior?

While Americans are very patriotic, they do not stand out for their sense of cultural superiority, at least not in comparison with national publics outside the Western world.

In a 2002 Pew Global Attitudes Project survey, 60% of Americans agreed with the statement: "Our people are not perfect, but our culture is superior to others."

This placed Americans in the bottom third of the 43 national publics surveyed, far behind countries such as Indonesia (90% completely or mostly agreed with the statement), South Korea (90%), Egypt (88%), Mexico (86%), India (85%), [the Republic of] Mali (80%), Uzbekistan (77%), Bolivia (77%), Tanzania (77%), and Bulgaria (74%).

Among the publics of Western Europe, on the other hand, there was even less inclination to assert cultural superiority than in the United States. Just 55% of Italians agreed with the statement; as did just 40% of Germans; just 37% of the British; and just 33% of the French, the smallest percentage among any of the 43 nations surveyed. (So much for the arrogant French!)

July 4th is the date we celebrate our birthing of a democracy—which, back in 1776, was a novel and radical form of government.

Not any more. The World Values Survey, which tests public opinion around the globe, periodically asks the following agree-or-disagree question: "Democracy may have problems, but it's better than any other form of government." In the United States, the last time that question was asked was in 1999; 85% of respondents agreed.

Sizable though that percentage is, it barely places Americans in the top third among the more than 80 publics asked that same question between 1994 and 2004. People in nations as disparate as Iceland, Bangladesh, Venezuela, Albania and Croatia all expressed even more widespread support for democracy than did respondents in the United States.

The Supreme Court Deprived Americans of the Right to Protect the Flag

Clarence E. Hill

Clarence E. Hill is the national commander of the American Legion, the nation's largest organization for wartime veterans.

One sure way to light up the American Legion's switchboards is for an overzealous homeowners association to ban the display of Old Glory within its community. While these disturbing incidents seem to be on the rise in recent years, I find it completely ironic that while a ban can exist on flying the flag of our country, no such ban is allowed to exist on desecrating it.

"Sorry, Mr. Veteran, you're not allowed to fly the flag on your private property, but the Constitution says you can urinate on it, spit on it, and burn it all you want," is what the government seems to be telling us.

The American Legion finds this unacceptable. In fact, for 21 years now, dating back to the Supreme Court's flawed *Texas v. Johnson* decision [1989] we've been pretty fired up about it. In that case, a narrow 5–4 majority ruled that flag desecration was permitted by the First Amendment. Essentially, a margin consisting of one Supreme Court justice invalidated flag protection laws enacted by 48 states and the federal government. The high court removed from the people the right to protect their nation's foremost symbol—a right that the people have enjoyed since the birth of this nation.

Supreme Court Justice John Paul Stevens and the late Chief Justice William Rehnquist usually voted on opposite sides, but they were both right about flag desecration. "In my considered

Clarence E. Hill, "Celebrate Flag Day by Protecting Old Glory," *The American Legion*, June 2010. Reproduced by permission.

judgment, sanctioning the public desecration of the flag will tarnish its value—both for those who cherish the ideals for which it waves and for those who desire to don the robes of martyrdom by burning it," Stevens said. "That tarnish is not justified by the trivial burden on free expression occasioned by requiring that an available, alternative mode of expression—including uttering words critical of the flag . . . be employed."

Rather than "free expression," Rehnquist compared flag desecration to an "inarticulate grunt," and wrote, "I cannot agree that the First Amendment invalidates the Act of Congress, and the laws of 48 of the 50 states, which make criminal the burning of the flag."

Constitutional Amendment

Fortunately, there is something we can do about it. [As of 2010] measures sit in both the U.S. Senate and the House of Representatives that would allow for a narrowly drawn constitutional amendment which would return to the people the right to protect Old Glory. It simply says, "The Congress shall have power to prohibit the physical desecration of the flag of the United States."

Flag protection amendments have passed the House of Representative six times in the past, only to fall short of the necessary two-thirds supermajority required in the Senate.

Flag Day during an election year represents the perfect opportunity to urge your congressional delegation to vote to protect our flag, the embodiment of what Gen. Norman Schwarzkopf called our "national identity."

While the Constitution is supposed to protect us from the tyranny of the majority, a strong case can be made that protecting flag desecration as free speech represents a "tyranny of the minority." Polls repeatedly show that Americans support this amendment. Fifty state legislatures have called for the amendment's passage. Overwhelming majorities in Congress have passed it in the past and the amendment fell only one vote short last time in the Senate. When is the last time that 66 percent of the Senate *agreed* on anything of substance?

Don't be swayed by phony arguments about desecrating red, white and blue neckties, underwear or beach towels. These are not flags. Would anyone consider putting these items on the caskets of our fallen heroes? Would you run a scarf up a flagpole? The beauty of the flag amendment is its narrowness—it covers the flag, not its likenesses. It also covers "desecration," not the respectful "burning" of it during its retirement, as opponents would have you believe.

The amendment is worth repeating: "The Congress shall have power to prohibit the physical desecration of the flag of the United States." Nothing more, nothing less.

By encouraging Congress to support House Joint Resolution 47 and Senate Joint Resolution 15, we can make the statement that our flag is important and that "We the people" matter.

The Flag Is Important and Should Be Protected by a Constitutional Amendment

John Andretti

John Andretti is a well-known NASCAR (National Association for Stock Car Auto Racing) race car driver. This viewpoint is his testimony to the US Senate Committee on the Judiciary.

I want to thank the members of the Judiciary Committee [US Senate Committee on the Judiciary] for holding this hearing. And thank you, also, for inviting me to talk on a matter that is of importance to me and the great majority of Americans—protecting their flag from acts of physical desecration.

By the end of World War II, my father's family had lost everything. He and his brother grew up in a relocation camp in eastern Italy, living there from the time they were eight years old until they were 16. They came to the United States at that point, a land of freedom and opportunity. And I am proud to say they made the most of it.

Sometimes he has a hard time describing it because of the emotion, but my father has told me about seeing that flag of the United States—first when liberated in his native Italy and, later, when "liberated" into a new life for him and his family. The flag of the United States represented goodness and freedom, and that is a lesson he taught to his children—and a lesson I am teaching to my children.

Being the father of three it is very important for me to teach my children respect and honor, not only for individuals, but also on a whole, and the flag is a means to that end. Our faith is our foundation, but there must be more, and it must be tangible, and it is found in the flag.

John Andretti, "Testimony Before the US Senate Committee on the Judiciary," www.legion.org, March 10, 2004. Courtesy of John Andretti.

This is obviously not my environment. I usually am wearing a fire-retardant uniform emblazoned with the colors of my sponsors and talking about NASCAR [National Association for Stock Car Auto Racing] racing. I am a race car driver, and have driven for more than 30 years—everything from karts to Indy cars to NASCAR stock cars. In fact, I hope every member of this committee will come join us at the track sometime—each one of you is very welcome. I know Senator [Jon] Kyl and Senator [Lindsey] Graham can tell you how great the fans are, and I know Senator [Joe] Biden, Senator [John] Edwards and Senator [Jeff] Sessions can tell you how much fun our races can be.

And they can tell you something about my bosses—the millions of people who follow motor sports in this country. When it is all said and done, every driver in major league racing works for the fans and, when you work for someone, you get to know them.

There are those who say the flag is only a symbol, but symbols are important.

I've learned a lot about those fans, as well as my fellow competitors and those who run our sport. I feel I am representing a huge majority of them here today. I am here because I fully believe in what Gen. [Patrick] Brady and the Citizens Flag Alliance are about.

I am very proud to be an American. Military or civilian, native or immigrant, the flag is our bond.

I fly the flag at my home, 24 hours a day. And, yes, it is lighted for all to see. I appreciate what the flag stands for and I know quite well what it means to the millions of Americans who follow motor sport racing. I think most of them would be surprised—if not, outraged—to learn that today, in our country, it is legal to physically desecrate the flag of the United States.

The Importance of Symbols

There are those who say the flag is only a symbol, but symbols are important. Just as it was a symbol of freedom to my then eight-year-old father in Italy and, later, a symbol of opportunity to him and his family as he entered this country for the first time, it had a message.

Race officials rely on symbols, on flags, to communicate with drivers during noisy racing action. Even with radios today, flags are still important and functional in racing. And in quite the same way, our nation's banner is important and functional, and still sends a message.

In NASCAR racing, you'll see flags waved a lot. But there is one flag that gets waved by NASCAR fans more than any other. And that would be the red, white and blue of Old Glory.

Early in our nation's history, the flag of the United States was something of a signal flag. Out in front of the troops, it signaled action by our military against the forces that might otherwise overrun us. It serves as a symbol of that very notion today as American troops defend our liberties and protect our interests around the world.

And burning a flag, it seems to me, is a very profound signal that those who desecrate the flag have total disregard for our military.

In 1967 Congress passed a federal law that prohibited flag desecration right here in the District of Columbia. Congress passed that law because of the effect that flag desecration had on the morale of the troops then fighting in Vietnam. That law, now made invalid by the Supreme Court, was the last show of congressional flag-related support for America's military men and women who are engaged in war. We should honor today's warriors and underpin morale by once again making it illegal to physically desecrate the flag.

I have to admit, I've never seen the flag burned, other than on a television newscast. Those I work with and those I work for—NASCAR fans—aren't the kind of folks who take to this sort of thing. Their flag is important to them, they respect it and they protect it.

I once heard a man say that the flag represents the freedom to burn it. I would disagree, and I think most Americans would, too.

The flag is a symbol that represents all that our nation is and can be. It symbolizes what the people say it symbolizes and the great majority certainly don't believe that includes the freedom to desecrate it.

Nothing tears down America more than burning the flag.

As a sign to rally for a cause, there can be no greater symbol than our flag. We rally around it in times of crisis, whether a natural disaster or a global conflict. Our history bears that out. The September 11, 2001, attack on America is a prime example of what Americans feel for their flag, and what they know it to be as a symbol of strength, determination and resolve for a free people to remain so.

Public Support for Flag Protection

The Citizens Flag Alliance and the American Legion have done a great deal of polling over the years. The figures are remarkable. Very consistently they have shown that more than three of four Americans want their flag protected. Honestly, I'm surprised the numbers aren't higher. I'm sure they are higher among NASCAR fans who are a pretty good representation of mainstream, blue-collar and white-collar America.

Some look at the flag and see just a piece of cloth. That perception might be acceptable, but their understanding of the flag's value is lacking. The bits of fabric that make up the flag are only cloth, but when you pull them together in that recognized pattern, something happens. As the flag, it becomes a binding force that holds us together as one people, and those who would desecrate it are out to break that bond. Nothing tears down America more than burning the flag.

I'm a businessman by profession and a race car driver by choice. But inside, I'm still something of a country boy from Bethlehem, Pennsylvania, where life is still pretty uncomplicated. To me, the need to protect the flag is easy to explain.

Events of late find us reflecting on the values that we believe are important and necessary in a free society. One is the right to freely associate—a major values battle now being fought by the Boy Scouts of America. One other is the right to publicly invoke the name of God in a patriotic exercise— another major values battle being waged by the American Legion in [its] efforts to keep the words "under God" in the Pledge of Allegiance to the flag.

As a nation we are bound together by our shared beliefs in such values. And we are bound by tradition as Americans to pass along to younger generations the importance of upholding those values that are uniquely American. One of the greatest tools for teaching values of respect, commitment, loyalty and patriotism is the flag of the United States. But how do you explain to a youngster that it's right and customary to respect our flag, but okay to burn it? I have three young children, and I spend time with children all over the country because of my racing activities, and I have no way to explain that to them.

What we are about today, what we are here for is important to all, I know. But what carries forth from here today is of greater importance. We are considering more than the just the flag here. We are helping to assure that the flag that flies throughout the nation is seen, treasured, and honored every day. You never know, it may give cause for a youngster to ask what the flag is for, what it means, or why it is important.

The answers, for most of us, should be easy. That flag is about values. It's about tradition. It's about America and the men and women who paid an awful price for what we have today.

We honor and cherish members of the armed forces and veterans of military service when we honor and protect the flag. Draping the flag over the coffin of a fallen soldier, placing a flag near a grave, or hanging a flag on your house on Memorial Day are all ways we honor and express our appreciation for those who have fought and died defending America. When our laws sanction the physical desecration of the flag the honor is diminished and the recognition is dulled.

There is importance to the flag as a symbol and one that has a noble function. In racing, your helmet is your trademark and mine is red, white and blue with the American flag as the theme. My "work clothes" are colorful reflections of the sponsors who support me. The flag has the same function for our men and women in uniform. For them, it is a reflection of the people who support them in their job of protecting all of us.

The American people deserve the backing of this body in their desire to protect the flag, and a constitutional amendment to return that right to the people is the only way.

For those who still can't see the flag for all that it is, or who hold concern for amending the Constitution we say, keep that concern. We respect your position, but please, please consider the desire of the great majority and move the flag amendment off of Capitol Hill and send it to the states for debate and ratification. Let the people decide.

Banning Desecration of the Flag Is Necessary and Has Nothing to Do with Partisan Politics

David G. Bancroft

David G. Bancroft is an author and the founder of the website USA-Patriotism.com.

I first want to point out a positive concerning the flag constitutional amendment failing by one vote in the U.S. Senate the last week of June [2006]. . . . It was the absence of the bitter partisanship that usually reigns in the halls of the Capitol building.

That's right . . . many Democrats joined all but three Republicans in voting for the amendment that would allow Congress to decide what action determines the desecration of Old Glory instead of the Supreme Court. (I am optimistic that the states would ratify it too.)

Now, about the failure by one vote!

It really bothers me knowing that some in Congress still do not believe the Stars and Stripes deserves special status that safeguards the flag against being burned or soiled in protest for whatever reason in the name of one's right of expression!

Yes, it is personal and emotional . . . and I think the majority of Americans agree with me. Nor is it about depriving anyone the right to express in favor or opposition on any given issue, as the purpose should not change if the flag is protected against desecration.

David G. Bancroft, "Old Glory Is America's Symbol," USA-Patriotism.com, July 1, 2006. www.usa-patriotism.com. Reproduced by permission.

For me it is about...

- Being a father of a son who served with the Marines in Iraq during 2003.

- Having never seen my mother's twin brother who was killed in Normandy during World War II.

- Seeing a flag-draped coffin.

- The lowering of the flag to half-mast when a president or another great American dies.

- Thinking about all the brave troops, including my father and father-in-law, who have fought with many dying or severely wounded to keep Old Glory flying ... and that is so wonderfully illustrated by the photo of the Marines raising it proudly on Iwo Jima.

- And so many more events and thoughts that just reinforce how I feel.

Feelings About the Flag

I know some might even say that being the founder of USA Patriotism! is the reason for expressing these thoughts. Well, USA Patriotism! is actually an extension of how I have always felt, which rose strongly to the surface on September 11, 2001, and with my son in the Marines. (I suspect the majority of Americans have similar feelings that are expressed more openly at certain times like the Fourth of July and Memorial Day.)

Moreover, how I feel about the red, white, and blue has nothing to do with politics. Ironically, it appears politics is the main reason why some want the ability to desecrate the flag, even if it serves to galvanize the silent majority against their goals. Oddly, I find it harder to understand and accept how others can say they don't want to see the flag desecrated, but just cannot bring themselves to give it the value it had until the Supreme Court's decision in 1989 [which ruled that burning the flag is a form of free speech].

I also have no problem with the flag being depicted on clothing and other products with the intent to exhibit love of the USA . . . and think that those who try to tie desecration to this use of the flag are ignoring common sense.

Then there is what the Founding Fathers would have specifically done in the Constitution about Old Glory if they really thought that one day long after they were gone . . . one could legally desecrate what most represents all that is the USA. Yes, these first great American patriots could have actually assumed after winning independence that the flag would always be revered without having to state so in the Constitution. And I believe they and the overwhelming majority of all past and present Americans would agree with my poem, "America's Symbol":

When you look up at me
with my red, white, and blue
waving proudly in the sky,
I hope you think about what I
stand for
beyond placing your hand over
heart
or standing at attention in salute.
I am so much more than
a woven cloth of stars and stripes
. . .
I am your pride of the USA
that is worn, adorn
and individually flown
for all others to see.
I am the courage shown
by the valiant troops
who raise me up
after a victory won.
I am the solemn remembrance
of the duty served to America

that is draped over a coffin
and given folded to a loved one.
I am each state
united as one nation
under God
with liberty and justice for all.
I am Old Glory,
America's symbol to the world
that will always fly high
in the land of the free
and the home of the brave!

May God continue to bless America and watch over her brave troops!

The Founders Agreed That the First Amendment Protected Symbolic Acts

Eugene Volokh

Eugene Volokh is a professor of law at the University of California at Los Angeles. He is also a contributor on The Volokh Conspiracy *blog.*

Congress is once again considering a constitutional amendment to ban the desecration of the American flag. The proposal, introduced this spring [2009] in the Senate by David Vitter (R., La.), and cosponsored by 20 other Republicans and Democrat Debbie Stabenow of Michigan, probably won't get enough votes. Yet even if it doesn't, one long-standing misunderstanding about the First Amendment is likely to live on.

Advocates for flag amendments argue that activist Supreme Court justices have twisted the original meaning of the First Amendment to protect symbolic acts such as flag burning. As Sen. Chuck Grassley (R., Iowa) said in supporting the Vitter proposal, "If you read the debate in 1790—the First Amendment was not written to protect nonverbal speech. . . . [W]e want to make sure we get the Constitution back to its original intent before the Supreme Court screwed it up." Or, as Judge Robert Bork argued in his book *Slouching Towards Gomorrah*, flag burning "is not speech," and the court shouldn't have held "that an amendment protecting only the freedom of 'speech' somehow protects conduct if it is 'expressive.'"

Yet the best historical evidence suggests Messrs. Bork and Grassley are mistaken. The framers fully understood "freedom of speech, or of the press" to include symbolic expression as well as verbal expression.

Eugene Volokh, "Flag Burning and Free Speech," *Wall Street Journal*, July 3, 2009. Reproduced by permission.

The framers were working within a late 18th-century common-law legal system that generally treated symbolic expression and verbal expression the same. Speech restrictions—such as libel, slander, sedition, obscenity and blasphemy—covered symbolic expression on the same terms as verbal expression.

Many cases and treatises, including *Blackstone's Commentaries [on the Laws of England]* published in 1765 and often cited by the framers' generation in America, said this about libel law. And early American court cases soon held the same about obscenity and blasphemy. Late 18th- and early 19th-century libel law cases and treatises gave many colorful examples: It could be libelous to burn a person in effigy, send him a wooden gun (implying cowardice), light a lantern outside his house (implying the house was a brothel), and engage in processions mocking him for his supposed misbehavior.

More than Words

This equality of symbolic expression and verbal expression was also applied to constitutional speech protection as well as to common-law speech restrictions. For instance, the first American court decision setting aside a government action on constitutional free speech or free press grounds (*Brandreth v. Lance* in 1839) treated the liberty of the press as covering paintings—not just words.

Likewise, in a 1795 Pennsylvania case, the prosecution and defense agreed that erecting a liberty pole was the sort of thing to which constitutional free speech principles might apply.

These tall poles, usually surmounted with a flag or a liberty cap, were originally a symbol of opposition to English government, but by the 1790s they had became a symbol expressing opposition to perceived domestic tyranny as well.

Protection of symbolic speech would have fit well with James Madison's initial draft of the First Amendment, which spoke of the people's "right to speak, to write, or to publish their sentiments." Courts and commentators (including early Supreme Court Justice James Wilson) routinely used "publish" to refer to publicly displaying pictures and symbols, as well as printing books. When Congress recast Madison's phrasing to the shorter "freedom of speech, or of the press" it was not seen as a substantive change.

The three most influential early writers on American law— St. George Tucker, Chancellor James Kent and Justice Joseph Story—all expressly characterized the First Amendment as protecting a right to speak, to write, and to publish.

To be sure, some in the founding era took a narrow view of free speech. They would have allowed the punishment— probably as "sedition"—of stridently antigovernment sentiments, likely including those conveyed by burning the flag. But they would not have denied that the First Amendment protects symbolic expression generally. They would have just argued that both harshly antigovernment symbols and harshly antigovernment words were punishable.

The Supreme Court has long treated symbolic expression—such as burning flags, waving flags, wearing armbands, and the like—as tantamount to verbal expression. In fact, the first Supreme Court case (*Stromberg v. California*) to strike down government action on free speech grounds involved symbolic expression (the display of a red flag). That was in 1931, hardly the heyday of liberal judging.

In *Stromberg*, the justices didn't discuss the history to which I point here; they viewed the matter as one of logic. But on this issue history and logic point in the same direction: From the late 1700s on, American law has recognized symbolic expression and verbal expression as legally and constitutionally equivalent. "Speech" and "press" in the First Amendment don't just apply to words or printed materials. The First Amendment protects symbols, paintings, handwriting and, yes, flag burning.

Flag Burning Neither Compromises National Security nor Indicates Treason

Julie Marsh

Julie Marsh is a former US Air Force officer and professional project manager who spent four years at the Pentagon. She is a columnist at the Imperfect Parent, *an online magazine.*

With Memorial Day a week ago Monday, Flag Day coming up a week from Thursday, and Independence Day next month [July 2007], it's an appropriate time to talk about demonstrations involving the United States flag—most notably, flag burning in protest of US policies.

For the record, I'm a registered Republican and a former military officer. I swore to support and defend the Constitution against all enemies, foreign and domestic. But flag burning is not unconstitutional. In fact, I believe that a constitutional amendment specifically outlawing flag burning would be unconstitutional.

In my research on this topic, I found a website that not only covers the reasons for my stand on this issue, but is a great resource for anyone seeking to understand the history and legal facts behind flag burning. Aptly titled "The Flag Burning Page," it's written by Warren S. Apel, "a political activist and writer, [who has] been running [it] for nearly 10 years now." As he clearly states:

"The purpose of this page is not to encourage flag burning. Nor is it to promote wanton desecration of a symbol which many hold dear. It is, rather, a standing protest to any amendment to the U.S. Constitution which would allow

Julie Marsh, "Flag Burning: Merely Incendiary, or Downright Illegal?" ImperfectParent .com, February 5, 2007. Reproduced by permission.

Congress or the States to pass laws against flag burning—
laws that the Supreme Court has already said are unconstitutional."

He began the page in 1995 in response to the proposed
"Flag Protection Amendment," which was introduced to the
104th Congress—where it passed in the House and was narrowly defeated—by three measly votes—in the Senate. It has
since been reintroduced twice more; both times, it passed the
House and was defeated by a small margin in the Senate.

Why would a military veteran be opposed to a "Flag Protection Amendment"?

---

*Part of upholding and defending the Constitution is to
preserve the essence of it: The Bill of Rights.*

First and foremost, because I support the First Amendment. As Mr. Apel put it: "We don't need an amendment to
the Constitution. In America, we don't put people in jail for
protesting against the government. That's what they do in Afghanistan, China, or Iraq."

And even more eloquent were the words of the State in
the Supreme Court decision in the case of *Texas v. Johnson*
(1989): "If there is a bedrock principle underlying the First
Amendment, it is that the government may not prohibit the
expression of an idea simply because society finds the idea itself offensive or disagreeable."

I love living in this country and I was proud to serve in its
military. I took my oath seriously—and in my estimation, part
of upholding and defending the Constitution is to preserve
the essence of it: The Bill of Rights. Symbolic gestures of protest such as flag burning are not worth prosecuting.

Mr. Apel's page provides a plethora of information in itself
as well as links to other sources of information. Apart from

objections to the proposed amendment on the basis of weakening the First Amendment, he cites other fascinating points . . . , such as:

- The word "desecration" implies that the flag is sacred, and the government (separation of church and state) can't say that something is sacred. (I'm sure you can believe that I appreciate this argument in particular.)

- Burning flags is "the only way to respectfully retire them. So when a protester gets arrested for it, it's not the *burning* that they're being arrested for. It's the thoughts in their minds at the time. In America, we shouldn't arrest people for their thoughts."

- "People who *do* burn the flag in protest do it for one reason more than any other: protest of anti-flag burning laws."

- "If I [were] arrested under the new flag burning law, the first legal argument I would make would be one of selective enforcement."

The Law Would Define "Flag" Too Broadly

Perhaps most entertaining is the point that if the proposed amendment were to pass, the federal government and the state governments would be free to define the term "flag" and outline punishable offenses as they chose. For example:

From 1947–1968 in the District of Columbia, the following language concerning the US flag was part of 4 USC Section 3: ". . . publicly mutilate, deface, defile or defy, trample upon, or cast contempt, either by word or act, upon any such flag, standard, colors, or ensign, shall be deemed guilty of a misdemeanor. . . ." That's right—expressing dislike for the colors red, white, and blue could be construed as "casting contempt" under this law.

In 1968, the code was amended (now with more legalese!) such that I won't bother quoting it here, but the definition of the term "flag" currently in effect in the District of Columbia is as follows: "The words flag, standard, colors, or ensign, as used herein, shall include any flag, standard, colors, ensign, or any picture or representation of either, or of any part or parts of either, made of any substance or represented on any substance, of any size evidently purporting to be either of said flag, standard, colors, or ensign of the United States of America or a picture or a representation of either, upon which shall be shown the colors, the stars and the stripes, in any number of either thereof, or of any part or parts of either, by which the average person seeing the same without deliberation may believe the same to represent the flag, colors, standard, or ensign of the United States of America."

Basically, anything that walks, talks, or quacks like a flag must be a flag. And if what you're doing to that flag or doing with that flag is construed as "casting contempt" upon it, then you're in violation of the law.

Most people don't want to burn the flag. Those who do are most likely protesting laws against doing so. It's a symbolic gesture that neither compromises national security nor indicates treason. There is no justifiable reason to commit our tax dollars to prosecuting and imprisoning citizens for speaking their minds.

Taking Away the Right to Defile the Flag Would Violate the Ideals for Which It Stands

Odeliah Dorko

Odeliah Dorko is a high school student who lives in Poway, California.

When I was attending my last year of middle school, dominating the campus as a mighty eighth grader, one of the mandatory courses given to us was U.S. History. I myself did not mind the course, as I have always had a special interest in the makings of our country, and it certainly did not hurt that I had a superb teacher either. One day, this teacher, a dear Mr. Swanson, handed out a sheet with questions that were meant to be a bit tricky and a bit more thought provoking. The idea was for us to ponder each question thoroughly and then to write out our thought process and conclusion in a semi-structured paragraph. While I do not remember any of the other questions, there was one that has stuck in my mind in the years to pass—does the government have the right to ban flag burning. Why or why not? The second I read that I thought, "Oooh! I know the answer to this one!" I knew the deep disdain and disgust I held for people who dared to burn the flag of my beautiful country of America, and I knew what my answer would be. However, when I sat down to type up my opinions, I found I did not know the reasoning behind my answer. I could find no constitutional reasoning that would allow for flag burning, a means of expression, to be forbidden. Far be it from logic to stop me when I want to write what I want to write. So, what I ended up turning in was a fiercely passionate and yet somewhat incoherent rant on the horrors

Odeliah Dorko, "Flag-Burning," RespectMyFlag.com, January 9, 2009. Reproduced by permission of the author.

of flag burning, and what should be done to those who would deign to defile the flag in any way whatsoever.

I am no longer in eighth grade. Over the years, I have found that I have cleared my head a bit, and am now able to admit defeat when all reason points to the opposing side; flag burning should be legal. There it is, I said it. Flag burning and any form of flag desecration needs to be legal.

Freedom of Speech Implies Many Rights

The First Amendment states, "Congress shall make no law respecting an establishment of religion, or prohibiting the free exercise thereof; or abridging the freedom of speech, or of the press; or the right of the people peaceably to assemble, and to petition the government for a redress of grievances."

Our Constitution was written to protect the ugly ideas which grate against our nerves and anger us.

The freedom of speech—what, precisely, does that term mean? Dictionary.com defines "speech" as "the faculty or power of speaking; oral communication; ability to express one's thoughts and emotions by speech, sounds and gesture." However, in relation to the Constitution, that word carries a lot more weight. [The philosopher] John Stuart Mill, born in the early 1800s, argued that "freedom of speech" implies three separate rights:

1. The right to seek information and ideas

2. The right to receive information and ideas

3. The right to impart information and ideas

Some may insist that this is a stretch of the term "freedom of speech," but if we look around at America today, we will find many forms of communication protected by the First Amendment, which are not, technically, speech. Bumper stickers, cartoons, television shows, pamphlets, protests, books, websites, organizations, and the list goes on. When it is obvious in our day and age, that the First Amendment covers all forms of expression—except, of course, hate speech and the like—why is it so hard for some to swallow that flag burning should be a legal form of expression? Is it because it hurts our American pride? Good. Is it because it makes us cringe to watch the beautiful red, white, and blue burn? Good. Our Constitution was not written to protect the lovely ideas, the ones which we can swallow with a smile. Our Constitution was written to protect the ugly ideas which grate against our nerves and anger us. If we take away people's right to defile our flag, then we are spitting on the very ideals that our flag stands for.

One last note: The last thing I would want to do would be to discourage the defense of the honor of my country and her flag. So, I'm going to end my post with a quote from Neal Boortz, libertarian radio host, for he has the right idea on such matters. "I would like to propose to the various states, a little addition to their criminal code. The crime in question would be 'kicking the crap out of anyone who makes a public display of desecrating the American flag.' The penalty for such a breach, I propose, should be a fine not to exceed 1.00 or five minutes in the custody of the police. Rights or no rights, I'm just not wired to stand by and watch someone burn my flag."

Organizations to Contact

The editors have compiled the following list of organizations concerned with the issues debated in this book. The descriptions are derived from materials provided by the organizations. All have publications or information available for interested readers. The list was compiled on the date of publication of the present volume; the information provided here may change. Be aware that many organizations take several weeks or longer to respond to inquiries, so allow as much time as possible.

American Enterprise Institute for Public Policy Research (AEI)

1150 Seventeenth Street NW, Washington, DC   20036
(202) 862-5800 • fax: (202) 862-7177
website: www.aei.org

The American Enterprise Institute for Public Policy Research (AEI) is a private, nonpartisan, not-for-profit institution dedicated to research and education on issues of government, politics, economics, and social welfare. Its website contains a number of articles on patriotism, most notably "Polls on Patriotism and Military Service, 2010," a detailed analysis on the results of many polls dealing with Americans' attitudes toward patriotism.

American Patriot Web

e-mail: headpatriot@americanpatriotweb.com
website: www.americanpatriotweb.com

American Patriot Web is a nonpolitical site dedicated to providing information, education, and other resources. It contains comprehensive information and/or extensive lists of links to other sites about the flag, American history, historical documents, veterans organizations, the September 11, 2001, terrorist attacks on the United States, and more. It also offers patriotic clip art and quotes.

Arlington Public Library

2100 Clarendon Boulevard, Arlington, VA   22201

(703) 228-5990

website: http://library.arlingtonva.us/departments/libraries/
sites/librariessitespatriotic.aspx

This web page, which is maintained by the public library of
Arlington, Virginia, contains links to many sites dealing with
the flag and other American symbols such as the Bald Eagle,
Liberty Bell, and Statue of Liberty. It also links to sites about
familiar patriotic songs.

Citizens Flag Alliance (CFA)

website: www.cfa-inc.org

The Citizens Flag Alliance is a broad-based, nonpartisan, non-
profit, national organization that was formed to persuade
Congress to pass a constitutional amendment that would return to the American people the right to protect their flag. Its
site contains editorials, congressional testimony, public opinion surveys, and background information on the proposed
flag amendment.

Flag Burning Page

e-mail: apel@esquilax.com

website: www.esquilax.com/flag/index2.shtml

The Flag Burning Page opposes the idea of amending the
Constitution to ban flag burning on the grounds that to take
away freedoms is contrary to American values. The purpose of
this website is to provide a rational and intelligent debate on
the issue of flag desecration, to illustrate the absurdity and
unconstitutional nature of any flag desecration law, and to assist students and researchers who are gathering information
on this controversial topic. The website contains essays and
links as well as detailed information about the history of flag
burning and of the proposed amendment.

National Foundation of Patriotism
1927 Piedmont Circle, Atlanta, GA   30324
(404) 875-0691
e-mail: admin@www.museumofpatriotism.org
website: www.museumofpatriotism.org

Formerly known as the National Museum of Patriotism, which was a physical museum with exhibits honoring American patriots and examining the meaning of American symbols, the National Foundation of Patriotism is an online virtual museum. Its mission is to teach, inspire, and motivate people of all ages about the history of patriotism in America.

True Patriot Network
1000 Second Avenue, Suite 3210, Seattle, WA   98104
e-mail: engage@truepat.org
website: www.truepat.org

The True Patriot Network aims to connect Americans who are interested in changing the nation's politics and culture and bringing them more in line with the progressive patriotic values. It works with a number of friend and partner organizations to promote true patriotism across America. It publishes *The True Patriot* by Eric Liu and Nick Hanauer, from which the last viewpoint in Chapter 1 of this book is excerpted; the entire book can be read online or heard as an audiobook.

USA Patriotism!
16009 Congo, Houston, TX   77040
(713) 466-5363
e-mail: patriots@usa-patriotism.com
website: www.usa-patriotism.com

USA Patriotism! aims to foster and display love and pride for America in a nonpolitical environment. Its website contains an extensive collection of articles, speeches, poems, photos, and music dealing with patriotism; submissions from the public, including students, are invited. Links to other sites with patriotic content are also included.

Bibliography

Books

Philip Abbott, ed. *The Many Faces of Patriotism.* Lanham, MD: Rowman & Littlefield, 2007.

Susan A. Brewer *Why America Fights: Patriotism and War Propaganda from the Philippines to Iraq.* New York: Oxford University Press, 2009.

Betty Jean Craige *American Patriotism in a Global Society.* Albany: State University of New York Press, 1996.

Alan Curtis, ed. *Patriotism, Democracy, and Common Sense: Restoring America's Promise at Home and Abroad.* Lanham, MD: Rowman & Littlefield, 2005.

Richard J. Ellis *To the Flag: The Unlikely History of the Pledge of Allegiance.* Lawrence: University Press of Kansas, 2005.

Robert Justin Goldstein *Burning the Flag: The Great 1989–1990 American Flag Desecration Controversy.* Kent, OH: Kent State University Press, 1996.

Simon Hall *American Patriotism, American Protest: Social Movements Since the Sixties.* Philadelphia: University of Pennsylvania Press, 2010.

Bruce Haynes, ed.   *Patriotism and Citizenship Education.*
Malden, MA: Wiley-Blackwell, 2009.

Steven Johnston   *The Truth About Patriotism.* Durham,
NC: Duke University Press, 2007.

George Kateb   *Patriotism and Other Mistakes.* New
Haven, CT: Yale University Press,
2006.

Stephen P.   *Authentic Patriotism: Restoring*
Kiernan   *America's Founding Ideals Through*
Selfless Action. New York: St. Martin's,
2010.

Lawrence L. and   *Patriotism for Grownups: How to Be a*
Eda J. LeShan   *Citizen in the 21st Century.* Victoria,
BC: Trafford, 2005.

George McKenna   *The Puritan Origins of American*
Patriotism. New Haven, CT: Yale
University Press, 2007.

Jan-Werner   *Constitutional Patriotism.* Princeton,
Müller   NJ: Princeton University Press, 2007.

Peggy Noonan   *Patriotic Grace: What It Is and Why*
We Need It Now. New York:
HarperCollins, 2008.

Igor Primoratz   *Patriotism: Philosophical and Political*
and Aleksandar   *Perspectives.* Burlington, VT: Ashgate,
Pavkovic, eds.   2008.

Robert Stam and   *Flagging Patriotism: Crises of*
Ella Shohat   *Narcissism and Anti-Americanism.*
New York: Routledge, 2007.

Woden Teachout — *Capture the Flag: A Political History of American Patriotism.* New York: Basic Books, 2009.

Joel Westheimer, ed. — *Pledging Allegiance: The Politics of Patriotism in America's Schools.* New York: Teachers College Press, 2007.

Lynne M. Woehrle, Patrick G. Coy, and Gregory M. Maney — *Contesting Patriotism: Culture, Power, and Strategy in the Peace Movement.* Lanham, MD: Rowman & Littlefield, 2008.

Periodicals

Michael Barone — "Spurning America," *U.S. News & World Report*, October 24, 2005.

Peter Beinart — "The War over Patriotism," *Time*, June 26, 2008.

John Branch — "American Flags as Big as Fields," *New York Times*, July 4, 2008.

Church & State — "Of Flags and Folly: Real Patriots Defend the U.S. Constitution," July–August 2006.

Bruce Cole — "Informed Patriotism," *Humanities*, January–February 2008.

Index